ALL YOU NEED TO KNOW ABOUT BEING A PENSION FUND TRUSTEE

2006/7

Andrew Freeman

" Since 2002 I have been in the odd position of being a financial and business journalist who is also a pension fund trustee. I rather fell into the latter role, thinking that it might give me some new insights into finance. Little did I realise that it was about to become a whole lot more interesting. I became involved in, and perplexed by, the debates that trustees have been facing to do with governance, funding and investment. There was a huge amount of information out there, but not much in the way of useful advice. And it gradually dawned on me that lots of trustees must be finding it quite a challenge and could use a plain-spoken and clearly written book that tried to tell them how to think about some of the big problems and issues. Essentially this is a book for trustees. But there are other constituents who might benefit from reading it – actuaries, consultants, finance directors, even chief executives. My goal is to help the entire system of pension fund governance to become more effective and efficient. "

Andrew Freeman

has been a financial journalist for almost 20 years, 13 of them on *The Economist*, where he has held jobs as varied as Banking Editor, American Finance Editor and European Business Correspondent. He is currently Deputy Business Affairs Editor in charge of the weekly back-half three-page special report.

Before joining *The Economist* he wrote for the *Financial Times*. He worked for two years on Lex, the daily comment column. Prior to that he wrote about euromarkets and stockmarkets. He joined the FT after two years learning the ropes at euromoney, where he was deputy editor of *Global Investor*, a fund-management magazine.

Author of several books and papers, he co-authored *Seeing Tomorrow: rewriting the rules of risk*, published by Wiley & Co in 1998. He also wrote "The risk revolution", a special report and survey for the International Securities Markets Association that was published in 2000.

Anyone with comments or questions about this book should feel free to contact the author at andrew@longtailpublishing.co.uk

WARNING

This book is a simple and concise guide to a complex, multifaceted subject that is changing all the time. Given the need to simplify an inherently complex subject, this book is neither comprehensive nor definitive. Readers must not rely on this book except as a general, schematic overview. Accordingly neither the author, the publisher, their agents, consultants nor employees accept any liability for any loss (direct or indirect; immediate or consequential; contractual or tortious) however caused from use of this book or reliance upon it.

This book is for Hazel Mills with whom I hope to draw a pension.

LONGTAIL

First published by Longtail Publishing Limited 2006

Tel: 020 7938 1975 Fax: 020 7938 3861 Email:info@longtailpublishing.co.uk

Publisher:	James Piesse
Sub-Editor:	Monica Kendall
Typesetting:	Louise Downer
Art Director:	Andrew Debens

Front cover picture of Robert Maxwell © mirrorpix

ISBN 0-9552186-0-8

ISBN 13 978-0-9552186-0-8

Printed by: CPI Bath Press

CONTENTS

INTRODUCTION

If you are reading this, you are almost certainly a pension fund trustee. Or perhaps you are considering becoming one. Or perhaps you are an adviser looking for tips into how trustees think about the issues you advise on. At a push, you might even be a finance director or company manager seeking an insight into how trustees think and behave.

Otherwise why on earth would you be looking at a book on such an apparently unexciting subject? Pension funds are boring, aren't they? And nothing could be more humdrum than the job of administering them as an unpaid trustee. (Only a few professional trustees earn money from their duties and they don't get rich.) If you think about the risk that you might be sued for negligence, and then think about the interminable meetings discussing how to communicate the tax implications of maximum sheltered lifetime allowances, it quickly becomes clear that being a trustee is not exactly a bundle of fun. It can be a frustrating experience. And in a rapidly changing regulatory environment, it seems that every few weeks there is a slew of new stuff to be digested.

In fact, I want to make the case that, for all of its occasional frustrations, being a trustee is an important and rewarding role. You are responsible for something that matters hugely to the people whose interests you represent – the safety and security of their retirement income. And whereas being a trustee was once rather unexciting, these days it can be surprisingly challenging and fulfilling. If you are involved in a pension scheme with a deficit, for example, the chances are you will be negotiating, sometimes tensely, at the highest levels in your company over millions of pounds in the form of recovery plans and contribution levels. You might be consulted by your managing director confidentially over highly sensitive plans for takeovers and dividends. You may well be in fairly constant communications with the board of directors.

The powers of trustees have increased by more than their status at present, but there is no doubt that the job has far more to offer today than it did as recently as a couple of years ago. And the message of this book is that, by using your powers responsibly and carefully, you can make a real difference. If you can be effective as a trustee, then you can carry out one of the most important, but underestimated, governance roles in modern corporate life. For that you will earn the eternal gratitude of the members of your pension scheme. And you never know, one day trustees might be paid as a matter of course!

This book is all about being effective as a trustee. I decided to get writing because I was growing perplexed by the changes in my own role as a trustee and somewhat dismayed at what seemed to be a generally low level of knowledge and confidence among trustees I met and to whom I talked. I was elected by scheme members as a trustee of my company's pension scheme in 2002 (typically, I was the only candidate!) and like to think I have learned a lot from the experience. But I have had to learn most of this as I have gone along. No one ever sat me down and gave me a set of commandments. The one professional training course I went on was little more than an overview, and presented none of the actual dilemmas that trustees face routinely. Worse, the sections that discussed investing were so amateurish it was embarrassing.

As it happens, the fund I represent has been facing many of the problems that have challenged trustees, not least the rapidly shifting regulatory environment. But I want to make clear that this book is not about my fund and it is certainly not about my fellow trustees, with whom I have been privileged to serve. For obvious professional and personal reasons it would be quite wrong for me to generalise from just my fund or to use any materials that are confidential to the trustee board and its advisers. That is why I have talked to lots of funds and trustees to draw out the examples and issues I describe below. It stands to reason that the examples are presented in a form that makes it impossible to identify the fund in question, unless there has been public reporting, in which case I have felt free to attribute facts or comments. But I repeat: readers would be quite wrong to assume that they can infer anything at all from the material below about the scheme at *The Economist*. The case I am making is a general one based on careful research.

So let me begin with some general observations about pension fund trustees. Most trustees are struggling to keep up with the demands of the job. Too often, funds are making decisions that are wrong or are deferring perfectly good decisions because the trustees are afraid they might make a mistake. Only a handful of trustees actually know anything about the biggest factors that determine whether their fund will sink or swim in the long run. Too many trustees are appointed by their companies and are terrified of being seen to cause trouble by questioning how things are done. They would rather sit there and rubber-stamp things than challenge something that might be unethical, dodgy or just plain stupid. Only rarely do trustees cross-examine their advisers and check whether they are talking sense and whether the fund is therefore pursuing the right goals. The quality of advice varies enormously, which makes it difficult to know whether to trust what you are being told. And many trustee boards are riddled with conflicts of interest that put all of the trustees concerned in very awkward positions.

And the amazing fact is that if you ask trustees about this, most of them will tell you they are doing a fine job in difficult circumstances. The difficult circumstances bit is true – it is much harder being a trustee today than it was a few years ago. But come on, it's pretty obvious that the average trustee is finding life quite challenging. You might have been persuaded by your advisers to conduct a "Risk Review" – a sort of survey designed to identify where your fund might be vulnerable to risks of various kinds. Sometimes these can be quite useful exercises, especially when trustees tell the truth. And when they do, one finding is extremely common, although it is not much talked about: one of the biggest risks facing most funds is the level of ignorance among the trustees. Most of them simply do not know enough to be effective at what they do.

If this sounds too harsh, ask yourself about your own knowledge and abilities. Have you done more than a cursory training course? How much of that did you understand, assuming that what you heard was actually correct? Go on, be honest: there are whole areas you are a bit hazy on, aren't there?

Actually that might not matter, it just depends on the holes. I went on one training course only to find during the afternoon that I knew more than the person doing the training. Now, I confess that there are some areas of trusteeship that I have deliberately avoided learning more about. One is the question of fund administration – you'll find some thoughts on this in Chapter Five below. I haven't avoided this because I am a total ignoramus and feel uncomfortable discussing it. Rather, I made a calculated decision. How much would it matter if a few glitches occurred in the processing and transfer of pensions and contributions? Obviously this would not be a trivial matter – it might be a sign that there were more serious flaws, perhaps even a fraud going on. Most likely, however, is that glitches will be caught and corrected. It doesn't need me to become a specialist in money transfer and clearing to tackle this. And the extra value I would create for the fund would be tiny even if my involvement speeded up improvements.

My feeling was I could add more value by identifying and learning about the really big issues – the ones with the potential to make a real difference to the overall health of the fund. In other words, provided I am satisfied that the specialist administrators who take care of the details are doing a good job, then I can think about the interesting and big things. (Some of these relate to administration – for example, trustees often have discretion on transfer values and early retirement policies – but are not directly administrative matters.)

That is my starting point as a trustee. What can I do to make a difference? And that is what this brief book is designed to help you to think about. I think I know how to make a difference. But to explain it to you I need to begin with some really basic issues.

Pension funds are quite technical and their fast-changing regulation even more so. If you want them, there are thousands of pages available that elaborate on, or challenge, my text below. If I have made any mistakes, it is entirely my own responsibility. But I have tried to be as careful as possible to make complex matters clearer than they often seem.

Whether or not you agree with me, I want to make it clear that I have not tried to be comprehensive or definitive. I am well aware that there is a complex and demanding recent history to the pension industry in the UK. It might be easy for a younger generation of trustees simply to criticise those who went before them, but often the reality demands more nuance. Often what looks stupid today was common practice a couple of decades ago among trustees, advisers and company sponsors who had good collective reasons for acting as they did then. What we must remember is that things change. And nowhere have they changed more than in the theory and practice of pension fund management.

I would like to extend my gratitude to several people who generously and bravely offered to read the book in draft form and whose helpful comments I have largely incorporated. One or two prefer to remain anonymous, but among the others I would like to offer warm thanks to Charles Cowling, Jon Exley, Peter Tompkins, John Ralfe, Norma Cohen and Cliff Speed. Thanks, too, to Martin Taylor for allowing me to quote in full his important NAPF speech. I never expected to write this book (I had much more glamorous things in mind!), so I must thank Chris Stoakes and James Piesse for their encouragement and support. Sincere thanks also to Bill Emmott, editor of *The Economist*, for his permission.

If you think I have got something wrong, please let me know – I welcome feedback and will certainly consider incorporating helpful comments into subsequent editions of this book. Please also let me know if you agree with me and have a telling example or anecdote that backs up my line. Like you, I can only benefit from the experience of others.

ALL YOU NEED TO KNOW ABOUT BEING A PENSION FUND TRUSTEE

Chapter 1

THE BASICS

SPEED-READ SUMMARY

- Trustees represent the interests of their pension scheme's members, not those of the sponsoring company

- Trustees should avoid conflicts of interest – these really exist

- Funds have different types of members

- To be effective you need to understand how your trustee board works and where the power is

- New trustees have to familiarise themselves with colleagues as well as a host of advisers

- Trustees have duties and liabilities, including a care not to be in "breach of trust"

- Trustees should communicate regularly and clearly with members

BEING A TRUSTEE IS MUCH MORE COMPLICATED THAN IT LOOKS

Sometimes when you're in the middle of a lengthy meeting and a pensions lawyer is droning on about the implications of the Pensions Act of 2004 it is easy to forget why you are there. What are trustees for? Why do we go to the bother? The answers to these simple questions are important. If you make a conscious effort to bear them in mind you will find that many aspects of being a trustee become much clearer.

So let's start with the most important thing: a job description. Your job as a trustee is to represent the interests of the members of the pension scheme. In the elegant words of the Pensions Regulator, "as a Trustee, your first loyalty must be to the scheme beneficiaries and you must always act in their best interests".

That seems a simple enough challenge, but it is actually quite complicated. And if you understand that complexity you begin to realise that the job requires some subtlety. Sometimes, for example, you have to make compromises and even sacrifices because you can't make everybody happy all of the time. Sometimes months seem to go by and nothing appears to have happened, despite clear decisions being taken at the last meeting of the trustee board. It can be a frustrating and rather opaque business.

I suspect that many trustees rather stumble into the role. Many are there because they have been asked to serve by their employer. Others feel some sort of vocation or want to be seen as good citizens. A few are genuinely interested. But unless you have been a trustee, it is quite hard to understand what is involved beyond the idea that you meet a few times each year to discuss running and administering the pension fund. As you may already know, the reality is quite a lot more complicated than this suggests. It is easy to be a trustee, as plenty of time-servers have proved over the years. It is, however, really difficult to be a good and effective trustee.

Of course, there is one reason why you should want to be a trustee: it is the best position from which to have some influence over the fate of your own retirement income. Until recently many people took that income for granted. Now it is clear that no one should be complacent about their pension. But there is no need to be supine either.

Think for a moment about what you are not there for. You are not there to represent the sponsor of the pension scheme (which is usually also your employer). In fact, until recently, you were not supposed even to think much about the sponsor – your only real concern about it was its intention to keep making contributions at the appropriate level to the fund. Not so long ago trustees did not even worry about that. Funds were in such rude health (or appeared to be) that many employers were able to take a "contribution holiday", that is, pay nothing towards members' benefits as they accrued because the fund was showing a financial surplus. It was not uncommon practice for there to be a compact between the employer and the trustee board to carve up surpluses between them, with the employer taking a contribution holiday and the trustees giving enhanced benefits to members.

That has changed, as Chapters Two and Six explain below. But this is an important point and I will come back to it in various forms throughout this book. Even if you sit next to your finance director and opposite your HR director, both of whom are fellow trustees, you absolutely must not fall into the trap of thinking that you have to toe a company line.

You are also not there to give advice to scheme members. At first glance that might seem to sit oddly with your broader mandate. But it makes sense. You are not a trained or certificated financial adviser, even though you might know quite a lot. You don't really have time to give individual advice, even assuming you were allowed to do so. And while you have some duties to communicate with your members, this is normally done on a collective basis and according to a regular timetable. As a member of a trustee board, you can't go around sounding off on your own, even if sometimes you might like to. Your goal is to be effective, and you will not achieve this by being (or being seen as) a loose cannon.

TRUSTEES VERSUS THE SPONSOR

Not so long ago, many companies did not particularly care about the membership of their trustee boards. Trustees were rather toothless and inclined to accept whatever their advisers recommended to them, and there was no difficulty in packing the trustee board with company nominees. There were some exceptions. During the 1980s, for example, there was a phase during which leveraged buyers often eyed up pension fund surpluses, launching takeover bids with the aim of grabbing the surpluses. For buyers and targets alike, it mattered who the trustees were and how independently they operated from their sponsor. Some target companies went to great lengths to insulate their pension funds as part of their "poison pill" defences. But, by and large, companies were content simply to pack their trustee boards with compliant trustees.

These days companies care a lot more about who sits around the table, and trustees face a far greater degree of career risk because often they have to debate matters that directly affect their company's finances. Chief executives do not take kindly to being asked for much higher contributions or to being told that they cannot make a special dividend while there is a big hole in the pension fund!

This is not to suggest that you need to adopt a hostile attitude towards your company. In fact, that would be damaging, because it would limit the scope for discussion and negotiation with it. Hostility is mostly unwarranted, too. Companies are not by nature dishonest or cavalier, and most of them are reasonably well intentioned towards their pension funds, even if they were rather quick to close them to new members and may now be trying to get rid of them altogether.

You will also find that whatever you think personally, yours is just one of the voices on the trustee board, and you don't want to be in a camp of one. It is very important that the trustees generally agree with each other or can have civilised debate over issues before reaching a consensus and moving on. Otherwise it is almost impossible for the board to function effectively. In some circumstances it might be appropriate for trustees to adopt what looks like a hostile position towards the sponsoring company, but these tend to be extreme. Again, look for more explanation in Chapter Six.

CAN YOU REALLY WEAR TWO HATS?

It might seem like I am labouring this point, but a few real examples can show just how important this is. Many trustee boards do indeed have the finance director and HR director sitting on them. It has become a sort of convention that these two company officers should be trustees, presumably because of their intimate knowledge of the company's finances and strategies. In fact, in a properly administered scheme, neither officer should sit as a trustee because in reality it is impossible for them to represent members' interests properly and impartially. (Cliff Speed, a leading actuary, points out that only a few years ago finance directors thought the pension fund was such an unimportant issue that there was no need to sit on the trustee board.)

How many times has a finance director had to switch from discussing how much contribution the fund needs to arguing that there is no way the company can afford the higher rate under discussion by the trustees? How many times have you heard the phrase "putting on my company hat"? We know that people find it extremely difficult to wear more than one hat. Strangely, then, many trustees have been almost routinely asked to accept that they can. You can see how this points to a subtle underlying tension between the trustees and the sponsoring company. That tension in turn leads to tension within trustee boards, particularly if the company officers are heavy-handed or make little effort to disguise their biases.

As John Shuttleworth of PricewaterhouseCoopers noted in 2004, "Everyone knows that trustees carry the hats of their day jobs into the meeting room. It is a convenient fiction that they do not – that is to say, the truth is inconvenient to someone."

Curiously, however, this is rarely spoken of. A refreshing exception was offered by Martin Taylor, former chairman of WH Smith who also acted as chair of its trustee board. We will hear more of Mr

Taylor and WH Smith later on in Chapter Six. But his relevance here is that he has been one of the few managers brave enough to talk frankly about the conflicts between his two positions. His considered take: "I was fooling myself that it's always possible to find an accommodation somewhere in between the two positions, and if you are doing both jobs and your left hand says 'A' and your right hand says 'B', you tend to come out somewhere between A and B. Often that's appropriate – but not always." Quite.

It is difficult to find real examples that show the extent to which this is more than an academic point. But here is one. In January 2005 Fitch, a credit ratings agency, issued a report on the deficit problem at many UK pension schemes. Although this was not the main subject, the report did discuss the growing issue of conflicts of interest (or as it delicately put it, "tensions between loyalties"). And some of the analysis is interesting because it contains facts that are rarely exposed in public. The report notes that "limited information was publicly available on the composition of the board of trustees at the other companies mentioned... " before showing the following table:

Diageo plc Pension Scheme Trustees

Trustees	Corporate Function
Graeme Forrester	Retired
Brian Higgs	Malt Distilling Director
Catherine James	Group Investor Relations Director
Ray Joy	Finance Director, Great Britain
Graham Logie	Site Operations Manager
Robert Moore	Finance Director Global Supply
Roderick Sivewright	Share Registration Administrator
Ian Shaw	Retired
Gareth Williams	Human Resources Director

Source: Company/Fitch

Imagine this kind of participation spread across corporate Britain, and you have a vivid idea of the scale and nature of the problem.

KNOW YOUR MEMBERS

These are themes that will recur throughout this book, which is why I have mentioned them right at the beginning. So far I have largely described something you are NOT there for. Remember I said you are not there to look after the company's interests. Your job is to represent the interests of the fund's members. That is not nearly as simple as it sounds. For a start, there are three different kinds of member, and not all of them share the same interests. There are:

Active members – members who are still employed by the company and who are normally paying contributions and accruing further benefits

Deferred members – members who have left the scheme or the company, maybe to work elsewhere and therefore to join another scheme, but who have not transferred their accrued benefits and stand to draw a pension once they reach pensionable age

Retirees – those who are drawing their pensions, a group that probably includes quite a few spouses drawing widows' pensions

Surely all of these members are in the same boat? Not exactly. Imagine your fund is in trouble. Its deficit is so big that your advisers say it must be wound up and there will certainly be a shortfall in its assets. Until recently, pensioners were top of the heap. Their benefits were protected as a matter of law before those of deferred and active members (though everybody is at risk of not getting their pension increases paid). The latter automatically become deferred members in the event of a wind-up. You might have first-hand experience of this, but it is a fact that in many schemes with doubtful finances quite a few employees (including directors who could see a train wreck coming) have opted to take early retirement in order to join the pensioner category, simply so that they can lock in their position at the head of the queue for payment. Any "haircut" (the term used for a lopping off of part of some expected benefit) will be felt first by actives and the deferred members and only as a matter of last resort by retirees.

In fact, I should make clear that this is a complex area that has grown more difficult thanks to changes in legislation and that is the subject of ongoing discussion among lawyers and pension specialists. It is no longer the case that existing pensioners get everything. Now only pensioners over pensionable age are offered first protection, and then only up to a maximum level set by the new Pension Protection Fund or PPF (see Chapter Six for more on this). In other words, everybody below the PPF minimum is protected, but only to a degree. The effect is a redistribution of wind-up benefits from pensioners to other members of the fund.

This need not be a huge problem. For most funds it is simply a piece of information, because wind-up is an unlikely event. However, think of it this way. If your fund has a big deficit, the ongoing demands of pensioners for stable inflation-proofed retirement incomes could be in direct conflict with the long-term interests of active members. As a trustee you would have to balance those interests and try to make sure that you were being fair to each category of member. For example, pensioners have grown used to annual inflation-linked increases. But in future these might have to be forgone in the broader interests of the scheme's members.

The important thing is that you act impartially when you consider the interests of the different classes of members. The same applies when you consider requests or petitions from individual members. You must weigh their case against the need to protect the interests of the membership as a whole.

Note: just to enhance this inherent tension, trustee boards often have one trustee drawn from the ranks of the retirees. This is odd because it is pretty hard for that person to represent equally the three categories of members. To complicate things further, this person is often also a former company official – say, the company secretary or occasionally the HR director – who may not have entirely shaken off the impulse to toe the company line.

APPOINTING TRUSTEES

I hope I have begun to convey the idea that it matters who you work with. And therefore it really matters how your fellow trustees are appointed and for how long. There is plenty of variation in this and each factor can affect the dynamics of a board of trustees. Among the obvious questions are:

How many trustees are there? Nine is a typical number, but some boards are bigger, some a lot smaller. On a smaller board a single trustee can wield more influence, but this can be for bad as well as good. It is usually a bad sign if one person is dominant. If you're in that position, then you should take steps to try to broaden participation and discussion. Remember that you are personally responsible for whatever the board does.

How are they appointed? Many companies choose the bulk of their own trustees, which is why there has been a heavy preponderance of finance directors and HR staff. They also typically choose the chairman of the trustee board, often nominating someone who is also a director on the company's executive board (or perhaps someone who recently retired from a senior executive position). Trustees serve for a term of office, anything from two to five, six or seven years. Sometimes this term is renewable, which is sensible if you have a good trustee who is willing to carry on, but which can equally serve to institutionalise mediocrity.

THE MEMBERS' VOICE

Usually some trustees are chosen or elected by the members of the pension fund. This is a good idea. If you have been elected or chosen by someone you tend to bear that in mind. You will feel more accountable than if you are simply doing a job because you have been asked to by the boss. In a typical scheme, one-third of trustees are chosen by members. The Government would like to see this move towards at least one-half and may bring in legislation for that purpose in the future. Take the case of a trustee board with nine members. If it has adopted member trustees, currently three trustees are elected or otherwise chosen by members. Under the Government's proposed alternative, that would rise to five.

Big deal? Well, again, it's a question of subtleties. Imagine things are tense and the trustees are wrestling with difficult issues as they try to close a funding gap or obtain a one-off contribution to prop up the fund. And assume that the member-elected trustees are gunning for this over the objections of the company-nominated trustees. Three of nine trustees are clearly in a minority and can always be outvoted by the rest of the board. True, the chairman represents the swing vote. But normally one or two trustees fail to show up at a given meeting, so a group of organised member-nominated trustees can be effective. Further, there are often clauses in the trust deed that governs the fund that allow for one or two trustees to call a special meeting. Used carefully, such clauses can offer active trustees a way to control the agenda.

Are you a member-nominated trustee? Then the above probably makes sense. If you are a company-appointed trustee, then you might bear in mind that your appointment should have no impact on how you perform your duties. Your responsibility is the same – to represent members' interests – as if you had been chosen by the members themselves.

If a vacancy occurs on your trustee board, don't just sit there and assume that the replacement will have the same status as the departing trustee. For instance, if the retiring trustee is a company-appointed trustee, you can ask for his replacement to be nominated by the members. If you put a formal request through the chairman to the sponsoring company, you might just get a result. But equally important, you will have sent a signal that the trustees are aware of the composition of the board and are actively seeking to alter it over time.

MAKING UP THE BOARD

Most trustee boards like a quiet life. It's human nature, really. Nobody likes unnecessary conflict, and running a successful board requires a collective effort, so it helps if trustees can muddle along together and avoid open warfare. Sadly, however, the introduction of new rules and the problem that many funds have significant deficits has meant that conflict has become more of a problem. Many trustees have found themselves in a position where they disagree with their colleagues, sometimes quite forcefully. This has put new importance on simple matters such as the composition of the trustee board – who gets to sit on it and for how long, how many votes it takes to reach a decision, who gets to call a vote, and so on.

Unfortunately, there is no single useful description of this that holds good for all funds. Part of your job as a trustee is to make sure you understand pretty clearly how your board actually works. After all, you can't expect to influence it and get things done if you don't grasp the basic mechanisms that you need to use.

A good starting point is to make a quiet analysis of the board. Who are your fellow trustees? Which ones are company appointees? Pay particular attention to the chairman. Is he a current director of the company's executive board? If not, is he a retired company manager? Is he a shareholder? What outside interests does he hold? Crucially, is he a member of the fund?

I am well aware that this might sound a little paranoid. Isn't it a bit much to assume such an apparently suspicious stance? Not at all. If you want to be effective, rather than just sit there and rubber-stamp other people's suggestions, you need to do your homework. And that means knowing who you can work with and who you might have to persuade or just outvote.

And the chairman really matters. He gets to decide a lot of things, from the agenda to what gets presented as the draft minutes of meetings, something I will discuss below. You need him on your side. So you need to know if he is a company outsider or insider. One trustee I know has an awful job because his chairman is a former finance director of the company and insists on a company friendly perspective, even though the fund has a very big deficit. Even though his arguments are sound, my friend only rarely wins because the chairman acts as an almost insurmountable institutional block. In another case, an active trustee has a good relationship with a chairman who is something of an outsider, even though he sits on the company's main board of directors. Because he is somewhat distanced from the company's executive management, the chairman is able to be quite independent and to keep the fund's interests in mind.

THE MONEY MAN

After the chairman, the next most important member of the board is the finance director. Frankly, his presence is controversial. How can someone who is intimately connected to the company's top executive management and whose job it is to run a tight balance sheet really represent the interests of the pension fund's members? There is such an obvious conflict of interest. Yet in most schemes it has been seen as quite natural for the FD to be on the trustee board.

Or it was until recently. When they rushed to close their defined-benefit schemes to new members, companies forgot something rather important. As new staff joined, they would be unable to join the DB (Defined-Benefit) scheme, but would be able to join whatever scheme had been put in its place, typically a money-purchase or Defined-Contribution scheme (see Chapter Two for more on this). This would apply whatever the seniority of a new hire. So if your finance director leaves, whoever replaces him cannot be in the DB scheme.

That raises the conflict issue to new heights. Can someone who is not even a member of the DB scheme, but who is a company manager responsible for shareholder value, even pretend to be an objective trustee? It is not a question of an individual's personal integrity, but simply one of principle.

Let me put the conflict another way. Under the new regulatory regime, trustees of funds with deficits have been urged to behave more like bankers in trying to get their money back. It stands to reason that the Finance Director cannot be a banker for the pension fund while he is also acting as the main representative of the borrower!

It is not surprising, then, to find that finance directors have been dropping off trustee boards, often attending trustee meetings in their capacity as company representatives, but absenting themselves from discussions that it is appropriate for the trustees to have with no company presence.

Where finance directors remain on the board and in the DB scheme there is still plenty of scope for conflict. At some big funds, the FD is asked to leave the room and has no vote on matters relating to, say, contribution rates or to the relationship between the board and the sponsoring company. This causes tension and no little embarrassment – no one likes to ask someone else to leave a meeting. But it is the correct way for the trustees to act so that they fairly represent the interests of members.

THE PROBLEM FOR BOSSES

We can take this argument to its logical conclusion. Trustees have a duty to ensure that their fund is fully funded. Failing that, they must extract as much money as fast as possible from the sponsoring company. In effect, they must push for a greater slice of the company's wealth to be directed to the fund. In theory, this could have a negative impact on the perceived value of the company for shareholders – some key performance metrics such as earnings per share would suffer if a big slug of earnings had to be deducted. And these are the same measures, by the way, that are used to gauge managers' performance and to determine their compensation. So an executive who is a trustee and who fulfils the role properly might have to take steps that would reduce his own compensation. That doesn't seem very likely, does it?

Actually, I make this point aware of the fact that it is slightly unworldly (it is what an academic would call "stylised"). In practice, transfers from the sponsor to its fund do not involve large shifts in relative wealth, indeed more often will involve little more than an efficient allocation of capital. Furthermore, although finance and HR directors are often trustees, it is much rarer to find a chief executive in that role.

WHO IS AT THE MEETING?

When I attended my first trustee meeting a few years ago I was rather in awe of the process. Around the boardroom were my fellow trustees, plus a sundry lot of people. Who were they? I had no idea. It turned out that one was the actuary, another a consultant, a third was the junior partner of the consultant, a fourth was a company representative who was there to comment on behalf of the sponsor, and the last stranger was a pension lawyer. Later in the meeting a new bunch trooped in to report on how they were managing £20 million of our money. It was all terribly confusing. In Chapter Four I explain what all of these advisers actually do. My point here is that it can be useful to tick off who is at your meetings. Do they really need to be there? Do you need to be more assertive in asking the company representative to leave the room when discussing matters that relate to the contribution rate? Should you discuss some issues without your advisers present? These are small questions, but they matter.

STARTING OUT

Becoming a trustee can be a slightly daunting proposition. One company that makes money by training trustees puts out a list of questions a new trustee should ask that runs to five pages and goes into an extraordinary level of detail. If every new trustee asked all of the questions the industry would grind to a halt. It seems to me a classic case of missing the wood for the trees.

A useful and much shorter list can be found buried in a booklet published online by the Pensions Regulator. It is so short it can be reproduced here. Among the questions a new trustee might consider asking, says the Regulator, are:

- Who are the current trustees and how were they appointed?
- Why is a new trustee needed?
- How often do the trustees meet?
- Who carries out the scheme administration?
- How are the assets of the scheme invested?
- Who have the trustees appointed to advise them?
- What powers and duties do the trustees have?
- What protection from liability is there for me?

Like any official list, of course, what is missing is the reason why you might ask each of these questions. Some are obvious. You need to know, for example, what the current asset mix is. But the first question, for example, is quite subtle. There is a superficial answer, and there is also a more in-depth answer, as I have argued above, which reveals a huge amount about the challenge you are taking on.

A WORD ON LIABILITY

One of the (many) reasons some people are unwilling to become a trustee relates to the issue of their personal liability. The regulatory position on this is quite fierce. But do not worry. The reality is that this liability is unlikely to be a real concern for you. Before I explain why, it is worth setting out the letter of the law.

Trustees are personally liable if there is a "breach of trust" under their watch, or if they fail to call attention to a breach of trust that occurred before they took up their positions. A breach of trust covers a pretty broad range of sins. It can occur if trustees take steps that are not authorised by the Trust Deed. It can occur if trustees fail to do things they should do, or if they fail to perform their duties under trust or pensions law. In other words, just about any failure, from a simple administrative error to outright fraud or negligence, can constitute a breach of trust.

This seems terribly scary, especially when you consider that you are liable for past sins and that you remain liable for any sins of your own even after you have ceased to be a trustee. Nor is your fate in just your own hands. Trustees have "joint and several" liability. Actually, that is appropriate – it reflects the fact that the decision-making on a well-run board of trustees is consensual and collective. But it does mean you need to watch your back. If you think your fellow trustees are making a pig's ear of things, you're right there with them when it comes to liability.

So why should you not worry too much about this? The reason is that most funds indemnify their trustees against any fines or damages that might arise from a breach of trust. It's called "personal liability insurance" and you might even find that this is built in as a clause in your Trust Deed. It means that unless you are wilfully and deliberately dishonest or incompetent you will be protected financially from any mishaps. Now, the Regulator notes unhelpfully that such indemnity insurance has "not been fully tested in the courts". But this seems to me an unnecessary caution. I think it reflects the fact that there are very few breaches of trust, rather than that there is a looming liability for thousands of hard-working and honest trustees.

HANG ON A MINUTE...

Not everyone might agree with my sanguinity on this. John Shuttleworth of PricewaterhouseCoopers wrote shortly before his untimely death in 2005: "Looking back, it is amazing that not a single trustee has been sued," so it is worth sitting up and taking notice. Is being a trustee about to become riskier? If we haven't been sued yet, is there a slew of lawsuits on its way?

Possibly, but today's trustees should not panic. Mr Shuttleworth was exaggerating to make his point, referring to the broad problem of the poor standards among trustees. He was starting from the observation made by Paul Myners as part of his review of the industry published in 2001. Mr Myners lamented the low standards of trustee boards and pointed out that bad and ill-informed decisions cost money – he even reckoned that pension funds collectively fritter away around £5 billion every year in the form of unnecessary transaction costs, which, if true, is disgraceful (and I will explain later on how you can avoid this at your fund). Mr Myners told trustees that they should "know their costs", but it was pretty evident that most of them had little clue.

What Mr Shuttleworth found amazing is that the members of funds seem to have done little to exert pressure on their trustees, and he pointed to trustee behaviour with regard to funding their schemes as a specific weakness. Again, I will explain this more fully in Chapter Four. I think the relevant point for today's trustees is that they should be steadily distancing themselves from the incompetence of the past. The more they can do this, and it involves making an effort to be more effective and accountable, the less they will be exposed to legal risk. To be technical, it is not necessarily a breach of trust to have been incompetent if the incompetence was a symptom of the widespread poor standards across an entire industry. Trustees alone cannot be held responsible for poor past performance. And if you are doing a good job today, you are much more protected against past sins.

COMMUNICATING

That said, trustees have typically been quite poor at communicating with their members, and this might have been in Mr Shuttleworth's mind when he wrote about lawsuits. Most funds send members an annual report, while the sponsoring company sends them an annual benefits statement that includes information about their pension. Increasingly the annual report is a summary document, the full version of which is available by request from HR (or is posted on the company intranet).

And that's about it. Very little other information is offered to members. And this reticence can cause problems. One fund caused a near mutiny when the trustees and the company made a joint announcement telling members that henceforth there would be a later retirement age and lower percentage benefits in future. As part of the bad news, the fund was also closed to new members. Not surprisingly, once they had overcome their initial outrage, members blamed the trustees for failing to tell them in advance that such important changes were being contemplated. If nothing else, members felt they had been denied the chance to lobby the company in an effort to water down the proposed changes.

My advice is to adopt a pragmatic approach to communication. Although you operate under a burden of confidentiality – you can't blab everywhere about what you discuss, which can often include intensely personal details about individual members as well as high-level debates about asset allocations – you should try to think about what might alarm your members and whether you can manage this by telling them in advance about what is going on. If in doubt, my instinct is to be as open as possible. But debate this with your colleagues.

ALL YOU NEED TO KNOW ABOUT BEING A PENSION FUND TRUSTEE

Chapter 2

TRUSTEES OF WHAT EXACTLY?

SPEED-READ SUMMARY

- Pension funds have a long history that trustees need to understand

- Today's problems have been largely caused by poor decisions and bad government regulation

- The aggregate deficit in defined-benefit schemes is huge and shifting

- Trustees need to remember that pensions are deferred wages that belong to members

- It is quite inefficient for companies to offer DB schemes that might better be provided by a specialist insurer

- Closing funds to new members has complex effects

- Defined-contribution schemes can be risky too

- Sometimes being a trustee can be stressful

I deliberately started this book with a chapter on the trustee's duty to represent fund members and the dangers of conflicts of interest. These have become extremely important issues as the debate about pension funds has intensified and there has been more scrutiny of trustees and their role.

However, if you want to be an effective trustee, then it helps to understand some other first principles. Why do we have pension funds at all? And why have they become so controversial?

You might have heard of something called the "pensions promise". Another popular phrase is the "pensions covenant". These are not quite the same thing. The promise is that the deferred salary that is your pension will indeed be met in future – you'll get what your company has promised. The covenant is an expression of the sponsoring company's ability (and intention) to honour its promise. The stronger the covenant, the more likely the promise will be met in full. If the covenant is weak, there is a greater likelihood that lack of funding might lead to a shortfall and a haircut for members of the fund – a promise broken. (See Chapter Six for a longer explanation of the covenant.)

As we saw in Chapter One, for decades there was no apparent need to worry about either the promise or the covenant. Most occupational schemes were healthy, or at least we thought they were. There were occasional scandals – Maxwell is the most obvious example – that occasionally called into question the integrity of the pensions system. But most of us paid into our fund without thinking very much about it. During the 1980s and beyond most funds invested heavily in equities and as share prices rose they sat on healthy accounting surpluses.

THE HOLIDAY OF A LIFETIME

Looking back we can see that this was when the trouble began. Successive Conservative governments worried that companies might be trying to avoid tax by paying pension fund contributions into funds that were already in rude health. So rules were introduced to limit the amount of assets that a pension fund could hold. Many companies thus took "contribution holidays". Accounting rules such as the now notorious SSAP24 meant that surpluses could be amortised through companies' Profit & Loss accounts. Aided and abetted by their professional advisers, companies also paid no contributions if their fund was in surplus by more than a set percentage of assets. In many cases, these holidays lasted for years, sometimes as long as a decade. So shareholders had a lengthy period when they had no rival claim on earnings. And trustees could not do much to argue that contributions should be paid or resumed. They were simply told by advisers that the rules meant there were adequate assets going forward. In some cases companies did make a gesture towards the fund, perhaps improving the level of benefits or bringing down the retirement age. But these were just ways of distributing the surplus.

In retrospect contribution holidays were a big mistake. Companies were not really trying to dodge taxes when they wanted to keep paying into their funds. Rather, they were sensibly continuing to pay into their funds because that was the right way to protect them from the long-term swings in financial-asset prices. Remember that most funds were hugely biased towards equities. When share prices fell, as they did steadily from the end of the 1990s, notional surpluses disappeared at an alarming rate, often so fast that funds moved from surplus to deficit in a matter of a few months. That was when the Government's rule-driven approach to surpluses began to look ill-judged. In reality, the surpluses would have acted as a cushion to smooth long-term performance of pension fund assets, if only they had been allowed to continue to build up in the good times. Instead they were capped and then diminished, so that funds were defenceless when bad times arrived.

This background is important for understanding where we are today. Funds tended to remain heavily exposed to equities. And as real interest rates fell along with stockmarkets, they moved en masse into deficit. The reaction by thousands of sponsoring companies was to close defined-benefit funds to new members and to set up parallel money-purchase schemes that offer new employees a much less attractive deal. According to the National Association of Pension Funds, by mid-2005 about 70% of defined-benefit schemes had been closed to new members, and 9% had been closed to further accruals by members.

APPLES, PEARS AND DEFICITS

How bad is the deficit problem? No one knows exactly because pension fund reporting is patchy as well as unreliable. For instance, if you are calculating a deficit, by definition you must value the assets and compare this to the liabilities. The trouble is that that second step involves making guesses, not least about the discount rate that is used to put a value today on tomorrow's liabilities (the higher the rate you choose, the lower the value of the liabilities today). So one fund might report a deficit of £X and another of £Y. Unless they have chosen the same discount rate, the figures cannot simply be added together to get a meaningful number. (I will come back to this issue when we look at investment strategies and the role of advisers in shaping them.)

This points to a very important aspect of pension funds that all trustees should grasp. Every fund is different. A fund will have a certain number of members of each category and hence a unique liability structure. It will either be closed to new members or remain open. It will have its own array of assets that will be different from other funds. It will have its own trustee board with a unique set of actors and interactions. It will have its own relationship with the sponsoring company that will depend on all kinds of human and material factors. We will come back to this in subsequent chapters. Of course, an important point is that there are similar issues and questions facing all funds.

But let's go back to the question of deficits. For those readers who are not trustees of funds with big deficits – be thankful! Your job is a whole lot easier because you can work from a position of being properly funded, with everything that this implies, not least a much more straightforward relationship with the sponsor.

Deficits vary in size, from huge to minor. Aon, an insurance broker, recently studied UK pension schemes and found that only 5% of them are fully funded – in other words, 95% of them have a deficit. (Interestingly, Aon says that in America 20% of schemes are fully funded and that employers there have been faster to address funding problems. But that could depend on different ways of measuring things and is another story.)

The best available study for the UK is done annually by Lane Clark & Peacock, a firm of actuaries. Trustees might be interested to look at this for themselves, because it more than repays a close reading – it's easy to find on www.lcp.uk.com. But it is worth summarising at some length its main findings, because they give a sense of how bad the problem is. That in turn sets an important context for the broader debate about pensions.

A VERY BIG HOLE INDEED

The Lane Clark & Peacock study looks at the pension statements of the top 100 British companies by market capitalisation – known in the City as simply the FTSE 100. For the first time in their 2004 accounts the 92 companies with defined-benefit schemes all reported their pension fund numbers using a new accounting measure known as FRS17, which appears on the balance sheet. FRS17 is both important and meaningless as I will explain later on. But for now it's as good a yardstick as any available for comparing the financial position of funds at leading companies.

The study found that the aggregate deficit of the companies at mid-July 2005 was £37 billion, down from £42 billion a year earlier.

That is a very big number. And it doesn't include some other retirement liabilities, such as those associated with healthcare and overseas pensions – if these were in the figures, the total deficit might be as much as one-quarter bigger.

The actuaries usefully put their published number into context. It represents:

- Five months' worth of the companies' pre-tax 2004 profits
- A year's worth of dividends
- 3% of the FTSE 100's market capitalisation
- Assets of £88 being held for every £100 of liability as defined by FRS17

Moreover, the actuaries point out, the reported FRS17 numbers do not tell the whole story. If a company tries to walk away from its pension liabilities then it must top up the assets so that the accrued benefits can be fully met by purchasing the appropriate annuities from an insurance company. This is an expensive option – if all the FTSE 100 companies with deficits went down this route, the shortfall would total more like £150 billion. Clearly that is not going to happen, at least not in one fell swoop. But the number gives an indication of the scale of the problem. No wonder it is consuming more and more management attention, and no wonder that trustee meetings have become ever longer.

BACK TO THE BEGINNING

There are various ways deficits can be tackled and I will come on to these below. But before then, let's go back to a question I asked at the start of this chapter. Why do pension funds exist? Obviously in this book I am referring to company pensions – the matter of state provision is a whole other can of worms. I have suggested simply enough that pensions are a form of deferred pay. Of course, they are more than that. For one thing, they have a privileged tax status, something that encouraged private (ie, non state-owned) companies to set them up in the first place. So employer and employee contributions are paid from pre-tax income. That's easy enough for the company. There are tax issues for employees, especially when it comes to retiring and choosing how to use the accumulated pension pot.

We tend to take it for granted that it makes sense as an employee to have an occupational pension, especially if there seems a good chance that it will be honoured in full by the company. But it's a good trustee training exercise to ask whether this is really the case. A bit of rigorous argument can challenge even the seemingly obvious.

Perhaps the most provocative thinker in this area is Jon Exley, a leading figure in the "new school" of actuaries. He is an interesting commentator because he has not been afraid to apply finance theory to pension questions. He was one of the first actuaries to advocate that funds should switch their assets away from equities to bonds, on the grounds that these best match the nature of pension liabilities (more of that in Chapter Seven). He is also a leading light in the movement to find capital-market solutions to pension funding. What does that mean? Well, instead of the conventional approach to funding a pot of liabilities, the capital-markets approach is trying to develop transparent insurance products. These can be used to create precise matches for liability streams, thereby taking much of the uncertainty out of the funding formula. This is at the cutting edge of pensions funding, and needs more explanation. But for now, the issue is whether it makes sense for companies to provide pensions in lieu of up-front cash salary.

SHOPPING FOR A PENSION

Remember that pensions are deferred salary. In effect they act as a form of forced savings designed to ensure that workers do not spend today what they will need to fund themselves in retirement. But what if, instead of deferring payment, employers simply raised salaries and left workers to fend for themselves? Instead of being told you have accrued a future benefit, you are given the money today to invest as you see fit for use at some point in the future. (This is analogous to the defined-contribution scheme approach that has replaced many defined-benefit schemes.) Is it more or less efficient for you to do your own saving and investing, or to have your employer do it for you?

How should we think about this? Well, says Mr Exley, imagine that a company chooses to buy its employees a fixed amount of groceries instead of some of their salary. Say, for the sake of it, it buys an identical basket of groceries with a retail cost of £100 for each employee. Because it is buying in bulk, the company pays a discounted price of only £95 per basket. The question is whether the groceries are worth more than £95 to each employee, in which case value has been created, or less, in which case value has been destroyed.

Now it starts to get interesting. If the groceries are basic goods that most (or all) employees would buy every week, then the answer might well be that the basket creates value. It is quite possible, too, that there would be a useful secondary market in unwanted goods, so that employees can sell things at only a small discount to the supermarket price. That would also help with the creation of value. Of course, probably the simplest way to organise this would be for the employer to organise a 5% discount for its staff at a supermarket.

Compare this idea to that of a typical DB scheme in which the employee has no exposure to the investment returns on the pension fund assets apart from the deficit exposure that would be triggered were the scheme to go bust. If the employee was instead paid cash of equivalent value to the pension promise, then he could buy a similar pension directly from an insurance company in the form of a deferred annuity – that is, an annuity that only begins to pay out at a defined time in the future.

OK, argues Mr Exley, let's go back to the grocery idea and ask two questions:

First, can the employer provide more cheaply the benefit that the employee could buy himself in the form of an insurance contract if the employer offered a pension instead of cash?

Second, if that is the case, is the value placed on this by the employee greater than the cost?

The answer to the first question is that it looks pretty hard for the employer to have an advantage over a specialist insurer. Perhaps the employer could contract out provision and use its buying power to negotiate a discount to the deferred annuity prices that would be paid by an individual buyer. But as with the groceries, it would be more efficient to negotiate a direct 5% discount on purchases of annuities.

ASKING THE RIGHT QUESTIONS

You might be thinking what any of this has to do with being a trustee. All will become clear. In the carefully structured paper from which I have drawn this section, Mr Exley describes "Stakeholder alignment and agency issues in pensions management". It's complicated stuff, but it boils down to an intellectual challenge to the very idea of pensions and how they are provided today. Given that trustees don't generally ask themselves about first principles, it's a very useful exercise to think through Mr Exley's ideas.

Remember the starting point where we said an employee could replicate the pension benefit himself by buying insurance. There is one big difference between a purchased deferred annuity and a company pension. The annuity does not include the risk that the employee's sponsor might go bust and be unable to honour the pension. It stands to reason that an employee, who is already unusually vulnerable financially to his employer because it is paying his wages and other benefits, might prefer a pension that did not carry additional financial risk to the very same employer. Assume an employer went bust or simply decided to lay off workers and the employee lost his livelihood. It would cushion the blow to know he had not lost his pension/annuities as well.

Mr Exley's conclusion is that there is no "convincing reason why employers provide pension schemes for employees, especially where the employer manages the pension scheme itself (rather than simply buying the benefit from a specialist financial institution such as an insurance company)."

Obviously this has big implications for how companies ought to manage their pension fund assets (see Chapters Seven and Eight) and Mr Exley has strong and important views on this too. But let's follow a different tack. You can argue that it is only a matter of time before such arguments are embraced by companies. Indeed, you can argue that by closing DB schemes, either entirely or to new members, companies have already signalled that they will not make similar pension promises in future. They have switched to a money-purchase system that puts the onus on employees to organise their own retirement options.

Before we move on, this is a good place to suggest a different way of thinking about defined-benefit pensions. In fact, it's an idea that has been endorsed by the Pensions Regulator, of which more later. But assume for a moment that a company with a DB scheme issues a set of pension benefits in Year X. Assume too that the company has every intention of paying up in Year X+30 when the benefits become due. What is the right way of thinking about those benefits from the company's perspective? Well, from the business's perspective, the promises are the same as collateralised debt, the collateral being the assets in the scheme that are put aside against full payment in the future (note that the amount of assets makes no difference to the value of the promise that must be redeemed). In other words, issuing a pension is the same as if the company issued a long-dated bond. The assumption that the promise will be kept is crucial – if it is broken, then, in effect, the company has defaulted on its bonds.

As John Shuttleworth noted: "Pensions waddle and quack just like bonds." And as the new regulatory regime keeps reminding trustees, they must act more like bankers who have made a loan that they want to be repaid.

WHEN A PROMISE IS BROKEN

Let's imagine a future in which company-sponsored pension funds are closing left, right and centre. The discovery by a worker that he or she is not going to have an expected level of income in retirement is an exact parallel of the homeowner or insurance customer who learns that their endowment policy is coming up short, often disastrously short, of expectations. Alternatively, what of the clients of a fund manager whose fund is down by 70%, but who continues to receive a handsome salary and bonus?

How do people react? There are lots of interesting consequences that flow from an apparently simple decision to close a defined-benefit scheme to new entrants and to switch provision towards a defined-contribution scheme. As in any part of life, not all of these consequences are intended!

First, the step is thoroughly demoralising for existing members of the defined-benefit scheme. Inevitably they wonder whether the next step will be full closure of the scheme, or some reduction in their expected level of benefits. Put another way, imagine a mature fund in substantial deficit. The only people around to make good the deficit are the active contributing members and the sponsoring organisation, be it a corporation or a public entity. But there is a real risk here. How can it be in the interests of the actives to stay in the fund? Unless the sponsor is providing a literally gilt-edged guarantee (remember the covenant issue from the start of this chapter?) that it will step up to, and remain at, the plate, surely it must be in the interests of the actives to divert their future cash flows into a new fund not burdened by the deficit of the old plan? This kind of issue is going to become more and more common as the industry struggles to solve its dilemmas.

Second, the sponsoring organisation in the future has two classes of pension fund members, and they don't necessarily have the same interests. As I have already suggested, there is a potential for major internal conflicts.

Third, if we accept the idea that defined-contribution schemes are unburdened by the paternalistic contract that is inherent in DB schemes, then clearly the employee will feel less indebted to the sponsor and more on his own. The contract changes from a paternalistic one to a hands-off one. The message to the employee is, in essence, "we claim no special responsibility to you in your retirement, and our responsibility is limited to giving you the means to make your own retirement savings decisions".

THE END OF THE ROAD FOR DB

What does this mean for trustees? It looks pretty depressing because the message is that DB is on its way out – the battle has been lost. Companies have concluded that the DB schemes are too expensive, so they will be cut back, capped and eventually abandoned in favour of DC benefits. A next, controversial, step might be for companies to stop any further benefits accruing and switch all their employees into a DC-style scheme. In effect this would accelerate the winding down of the DB sector. The NAPF has gone so far as to predict that DB schemes will disappear from the private sector within five years.

It is predictions like that that drove one distinguished columnist to fire off perhaps the sharpest denunciation to date of Britain's pensions system. Martin Wolf, long a commentator on the *Financial Times*, accused companies of being "deceitful" and successive governments of being "irresponsible" when he wrote about what he called a "shameful pensions confidence trick". "What we are watching", he wrote, "is the unwinding of what was – in effect, if not in intention – a confidence trick known as 'bait and switch': offer something attractive and then switch it for something else when the customer comes to collect." In a couple of short paragraphs he summed up how companies succumbed to the temptation to make the switch. For example, he noted, schemes designed to suit employers' interests would extract resources from less valuable workers such as early leavers – which they did. "Above all, they should make a credible promise to pay, but have ways of avoiding doing so when the bulk of those obligations come due." He lambasted actuaries for rubber-stamping companies' decision to gamble on risky assets. And he concluded: "Everybody involved should feel thoroughly ashamed of themselves." Amen to that.

SOME THOUGHTS ON DC

A popular and much-cited perception is that DC schemes transfer investment risk from the employer to the employee. Read around the pensions literature, and you will find that this is something of a cliché. But, as Charles Cowling of Mercer Consulting and others have pointed out, this idea is quite wrong. First, it starts from the incorrect assumption that investment risk in DB schemes is naturally borne by the employer. But this need not be the case – it is quite possible for a fund sponsor to immunise a DB fund against investment risk. The perception arises because most funds have deliberately mismatched their assets and liabilities, normally at the behest of the sponsor. But the sponsor is really only taking that risk if it genuinely intends to honour its promises if things go wrong. In other words, investment risk is only with the employer while the employer wants it to be. DB schemes are inherently much riskier than the common view has it.

There is a second massive assumption built into the common view: that DC involves the members taking risk. It is true that DC schemes leave it up to individual members to make their investment choices. Some schemes keep it simple, offering a very narrow choice of, say, an equity tracker fund, a bond fund, cash and typically a "lifestyle" option (if you don't know what this is, you should – it's an investment vehicle that supposedly reduces risk by shifting its asset allocation gradually from equities to bonds as the holder moves towards retirement age). Other schemes offer a panoply of choice, assuming a much greater degree of investment sophistication among the members. Few, however, give members the option to buy deferred annuities, which would arguably be the safest way to build up a pension.

So is this inherently riskier? Mr Cowling argues pretty persuasively that it need not be. A member could choose to take nearly no risk at all, buying deferred annuities. The fact is that most members choose to take risk, and lots of it, loading up on equities in a bizarre parallel to their now closed DB schemes. Does this make sense? Surely the vast majority of members should ask themselves whether their retirement fund is an appropriate vehicle in which to take risk? Maybe they would be better off taking as little risk as possible, thereby increasing the certainty that they will enjoy a minimum safety net in their old age?

So let's knock the "DC risky for members – DB not risky for members" idea on its head. Either fund arrangement can be as risky or riskless as those who run it decide. When you grasp that, a whole lot of other issues related to pensions and pensions management are much easier to understand.

REASONS TO BE CHEERFUL

Actually, it's not quite as depressing as that. First, the DB schemes will take a long time to wind down, so there will be a long-term challenge for trustees whatever happens. Depending on an individual fund's demographics, it might be another 50 or 60 years before the last pensioner or dependant dies. If longevity continues to improve it might be another 80 or even 90 years, assuming the last members into funds before they were closed could have been in their early twenties. So: the DB pot is worth fighting for. A trustee would be failing in his duty if he simply gave in.

Second, too few trustees have put their brains to work as to how they should fight for the DB pot. It is partly a question of extracting as much money as possible from the sponsor so that the fund is as close to being fully funded as possible. But it's also a matter of understanding the characteristics of a closed fund. They differ subtly from those of a fund that has remained open to new members. Once you close a fund, you shut the door to the new entrants that top up the population pool from the bottom. You take away from the fund that vital element of refreshment. Instead, the fund begins a long, slow, but inevitable wind-down, until eventually it reaches the point where the trustees are managing a dwindling pool of assets for a few remaining beneficiaries, and are hoping like mad that the assets will stretch far enough. (If the trustees have done their job, that should be the case, indeed there should be a small residual fund to see out the winding-up process.)

That has big implications for trustees. You have certainty about the wind-up as the fund's liabilities tail off – you know it has to happen eventually. So it follows that you require more, and ideally symmetrical, certainty in the fund's assets. You would move naturally towards a more conservative stance, wanting to take less and less risk that there will be an ultimate shortfall.

Isn't that obvious? Well, actually, it's quite a radical view and there are plenty of professional advisers who might dispute the above logic. My point is that these advisers are not trustees and therefore do not have the same point of view, so you should take what they say with a pinch of salt. I'm only guessing at what companies might do, but the signs that they will continue to be committed to DB schemes are few and far between. It's not uncommon to find top company managers who will admit in private that it was a mistake made in a hurry when they closed the DB schemes to new members. It helped to crystallise the very problems they have to deal with today. Equally, it's not uncommon to find managers who are willing to contemplate taking the big step of closing their DB schemes entirely.

THE CONSEQUENCES OF CLOSURE

Another awkward problem arises from the closure to new members of DB schemes, and this should have been foreseen. The fact that it wasn't speaks volumes about the unintended consequences that have followed the DB closures. The example that follows of a medium-sized fund is based on a real case. Two years after the DB scheme was closed to new members there was a round of cost-cutting, with the result that 800 staff out of 5,000 were laid off, most of them becoming deferred pensioners, but a few taking early retirement.

Now, when someone moves to deferred status, guess what happens? The fund no longer receives their or their employer's contributions. Typically it is the longest-serving and highest-paid workers who are laid off, so the effect is to reduce the overall contribution level significantly (the flipside is that these members accrue no further benefits). At the same time, it is not long before the deferred members will start to draw their pensions. From the fund's perspective, this is a double whammy – less money coming in, and very soon a lot more going out. In other words, unexpected events, such as a faster tailing off of active members, can have very nasty consequences, especially when the fund is already in large deficit (as this one was).

I suggested that this was unforeseen. In fact, the likelihood that there would be a decline in the number of active members was foreseen by the fund's actuary and investment consultants. They explicitly mentioned it as a risk factor as part of their triennial review and analysis, just one year before the mass departure of members. But the actuary and advisers thought the fall in active membership would take place gradually and steadily, and they therefore modelled it that way. This proved to be deeply misleading for the trustees (and for the sponsoring company, in fact, because it was forced to scramble too once the true numbers became apparent).

What should trustees do in this circumstance? Their first step should be to talk with their actuary and ask him to model the impact of the departures. Then it might be appropriate to have urgent talks with the sponsoring company. I will explain more in Chapter Five some of the options open to trustees in this kind of extreme circumstance.

(A theoretical note is needed here. It might not be fully obvious, but it is worth explicitly pointing out that the actual fact of closing a fund to new members does not in itself cause a problem. Indeed, as Cliff Speed has pointed out, the very idea of a dependence on active members to keep a fund going assumes a sort of generational cross-subsidy – something that sits awkwardly with trustees' duty to look after each class of member. The real issue is the same as it always is: do you have sufficient assets to cover the fund's accrued liabilities? The answer to that is typically calculated using your actuary's assumptions, and it is into these that demographic assumptions are built. In other words, the closure effect I have just described is one caused by your actuary.)

It should be clear by now that there is plenty for trustees to think about before they start worrying over what percentage of equities to hold. The more you understand the background to the pension promise and how it has been evolving, the more effectively you will be able to identify the issues that most affect your fund and that have the most scope for action. What does your fund look like? How does its situation compare to that of other funds? What is the covenant between the trustees and the company? Might something change it in future that can be foreseen?

WHAT TO DO ABOUT STRESS?

You might conclude that all of this is just going to give you a headache. Actually, stress is an issue for trustees and it is rarely mentioned. But I should discuss it. I know plenty of trustees who find the job increasingly stressful. One obvious cause is the growing weight of regulation and oversight, which makes people feel that they are at risk of being judged incompetent.

Another is that as trustees have been given more powers, with the expectation that they will use them, so they have been forced into more conflictual relations with their sponsoring company, which, as we know, is usually their employer. It is quite stressful to argue about deferred pay with the very body that is paying you today.

Another source of stress comes when there is a divide on the trustee board itself, often between a minority who want to make a difference and are prepared to push hard to get what they want and a majority that is far more reluctant to challenge the sponsor or to address any conflicts of interest that might exist. As I said above, it's not a nice thing to have to ask a colleague to leave the room. Nor is it very pleasant to have colleagues questioning each other's motives or wondering privately whether a fellow trustee is conflicted.

Let me comment on one other big source of stress that is almost a taboo because it receives hardly any attention: the membership. Yes, your very own fund members cause you stress, even if you are not always aware of it. The reason is that they take little interest in what you are doing until they think that something has gone wrong. Then they do not hesitate to blame the trustees, even if there was little in practice the board could do. Let me give an example. One company had a generous DB pension scheme as a hangover from the days of contribution holidays – as a sop to employees, terms had been sweetened while the company scaled back its contributions for a decade. When times became tough, the company made a unilateral decision to take back the extra benefits and return to the previous regime, while also closing the scheme to new members. It did not consult the trustees, except to tell them as a courtesy a day before the new deal was announced. (Under the law, by the way, it had no obligation to consult them, though this is now to change.) When the announcement was made there was mayhem. Staff were shocked and angered, and they quickly focused their anger on the trustees. Why hadn't they stepped in? Worse, why had they said nothing to members about the forthcoming changes? Of course, the trustees had been powerless, but that did not stop the members from feeling betrayed and upset. Several of the trustees, including ironically a couple of member-nominated trustees, resigned a few months later.

Sadly there is not much that can be done about this. The job is stressful if it's done properly. It might help if trustees were paid – I know I have sometimes felt that I am doing a huge amount of work for no measurable return. But pay might actually increase stress because it would raise the expectation that you will achieve something positive, whereas for perfectly good reasons you might not. It's a complicated area. But I think it helps to name the beast – you are better off accepting that there is some degree of stress than remaining in denial.

TWIN-TRACK TRUSTEES

In the world before the pensions crisis, it was not especially stressful to be a trustee. In fact, if you ask colleagues who acted as trustees in the 1980s it was rather jolly. Meetings were relaxed and the biggest issue they addressed was whether to hire or fire their investment managers.

That has all changed. And one aspect of change is worth mentioning. As DB funds have been closed to new members, sponsoring companies have typically set up DC schemes that serve people joining the company. These funds are far more straightforward and they face far less complex issues. But they also bring with them a headache. Has your company set up a separate board of trustees for the new scheme, or is it running both in parallel using the same set of trustees? The answer matters.

If it is positive, ie, there is a separate board, then fine. If not, you need to think about the implications for the DB scheme. If you are a DB trustee, then it is highly unlikely that you are a member of the DC scheme (the few exceptions may be senior company managers who have recently joined and are placed on the trustee board despite the apparent conflict of interest). By itself that is not a big problem. At this stage most DC schemes are quite small and they do not yet raise especially complicated issues. As they grow that will change and trustees will have to wrestle with some tricky questions, notably on how much choice of investment vehicle they should or must offer to members.

No, the real issue concerns who is paying for what. Think about it. The scheme foots the bill for all the advice that is sought from experts, and the bill is not small. But it is not in the interests of the DB members to spend a penny on the business of the DC scheme and as a trustee you can probably see straightaway that you should be quite uncomfortable with this idea. Yet in many schemes, because they are running in parallel, there is often DC business conducted during the DB trustee board's meeting. Unless some explicit arrangement has been made that allocates costs according to time, the DB members are in effect subsidising the DC members.

Of course, this being the world of trustees and conflicts of interest, there are very few boards that have tackled this rather thorny issue. I know of one trustee who resigned because she found the conflict of interest too much to bear when her fund introduced a DC section and expected her to be a trustee of both DB and DC funds.

What should you do? Well, if you recognise this problem, you ought to raise it at your next trustee meeting. Logically, the DC section should be billed separately from the DB scheme so that the costs of running it are borne by those who benefit. In practice, the costs are often blurred so that it is impossible to strip out the DC element. One of your duties as a trustee is to monitor the costs of your advisers and administrators, so you are perfectly within your rights to raise the issue of overall costs and how they are allocated. And as the DB scheme winds down while the DC section grows, this issue will become more relevant rather than less.

ALL YOU NEED TO KNOW ABOUT BEING A PENSION FUND TRUSTEE

Chapter 3

OK, THERE ARE SOME BORING BITS

SPEED-READ SUMMARY

■ The Pensions Regulator has issued lots of helpful guidance for trustees

■ Don't be too intimidated by the requirement for knowledge and understanding – yet

■ Focus on the big issues and responsibilities

■ Trustees must read and understand the Trust Deed that governs their fund

■ This will tell you what powers you have

■ Minutes of meetings can be a powerful tool for getting things done and for reporting back to members, so trustees should use them

If you have read the first two chapters, then you will probably not need much more explanation for why it is rumoured that DB trustees have been resigning in droves, or for why those who remain are both stressed and a bit befuddled. The job is so much more complicated than it used to be. And it's getting ever more complicated. Regulation is piling on the pressure. That said, the rush of resignations is just a rumour: trustee boards naturally have turnover. No one knows for sure, because no one monitors, whether there has actually been an increase in the rate of resignations. The real point is that the job has become both more challenging and more interesting.

Remember, though, that you can make a difference. And you can fight your way through the thickets of advice and regulation. It's a matter of knowing what questions to ask and what actions to take. So far I have suggested a range of practical issues in Chapter One and some more theoretical questions in Chapter Two. I hope I have raised things that every reader can relate to – they are things that crop up everywhere, so they should be familiar, even if you have never thought about them exactly the way I have suggested.

Now I am going to turn to a few areas that, on the surface at least, appear to be deadly boring. Given that what I have discussed so far has been quite lively and interesting it seems a shame to have a chapter on boring bits. But please read on. I'll keep it as brief and un-boring as possible.

Let's start with regulation. There are thick books on this subject, weighty tomes that keep lawyers busy but have little direct relevance to your work. Unless you are turned on by such texts, ignore them, you absolutely do not have to read them. There are also lots of glossy publications, some of them from actual regulators, others from associations like the NAPF, still others from law firms, actuaries and consultants. Read them if you want to, and occasionally you might learn something or you might find that your memory is usefully refreshed. But in general these publications are too dry to be of much use. They don't, as it were, call a deficit a gaping great hole.

There is one important exception, however. The relatively new Pensions Regulator has issued a set of guidelines for trustees that have greatly shaken up the entire pensions industry (these are discussed in Chapter Six). Reading and understanding the guidelines is essential if you are to be an effective trustee (and they will soon be followed by some e-learning options on the Pensions Regulator's website). If you don't have a good sense of the guidelines and what they mean, then you will struggle to be really effective.

But my main point here is that for most practical purposes you can afford to ignore large swathes of regulation. This is not a very politically correct position. You might even think it is in direct contradiction to the advice you have been given by your lawyers or by the consultants who advise you. Surely every trustee has to know the rules quite thoroughly?

Well, in theory, yes. I know of one fund which, on the recommendation of its advisers, conducted a risk review – if you recall, I mentioned this practice in my Introduction. Essentially this involves a trained outsider interviewing trustees individually across a whole range of issues. By asking them questions, the reviewer can ascertain where there are gaps in each trustee's knowledge and can then advise them on which training courses or conferences might be useful in future. By putting all of those gaps together, the reviewer can also give feedback to the board. There might be areas where every trustee is weak, for example, so urgent training would be required. In practice, of course, a trustee board reflects the different strengths and weaknesses of the trustees. Some know more about investment, while others prefer to concentrate on administrative procedures. What really matters is whether the collective knowledge of the board is up to scratch.

The fund I am referring to was initially alarmed when it received its risk review. It appeared that with one exception the trustees were indeed woefully ignorant about the precise laws and regulations governing pension funds. Surely, worried the sponsoring company, this meant the trustee board might be in breach of its duty? Well, hang on. Let's be realistic. It is impossible for every individual to be an expert on pensions regulation. There is simply too much complexity and too little time is available to get to grips with it. Plus the payback from becoming an expert is minimal unless you want to retrain as a lawyer. What matters is that the board is well informed about the basics. And knows when to ask for professional advice.

So let's also be practical. By all means go on a training course if you feel the need. Much more importantly, you have professional advisers who are paid to be experts on regulation. Use them. They will soon tell you what you can and cannot do under the rules. And if you think your sponsor is breaking the rules, you can ask the experts' advice. If you take their counsel, you are doing your duty. If you doubt their counsel, you are also doing your duty and you might want to seek a second opinion, much as you would if you doubted your doctor.

THE TRUSTEE AS WALKING ENCYCLOPEDIA

It is worth elaborating on the point that trustees cannot be expected to be experts on everything. In fact, the law is pushing in the direction of requiring more expertise – one reason why trustees have been urged to work harder and why there is a nascent bull market in independent trustees who supposedly know more about what they are doing.

But again I think it's a matter of being realistic. You want to be an effective trustee. And you can achieve that by improving your knowledge and learning to ask the right questions. You absolutely cannot achieve that by having a scatter-gun approach to learning, however, and that is sometimes what it seems the Government wants. You will do much better if you focus your efforts. You might even discuss this with your fellow trustees. It would be perfectly reasonable for some of them to focus their efforts on administrative matters while you and a couple of colleagues paid more attention to investments, for example.

My point is that you should not be put off from becoming a trustee by a sense that you don't know enough. Nor should you feel that you must spend all of your time attending training courses on the implications of the Pensions Act just to make sure that no one can accuse you of being an ignoramus.

TRUST IN THE TRUST DEED

I implied in the Introduction that most trustees have been doing a lousy job. That might seem a bit harsh. But it's time to face up to one of the industry's dirty little secrets. Trustees are governed by trust law. Why? Well, the original idea was to make sure that the assets of the pension fund were entirely separated from those of the sponsoring employer. In other words, a Trust would protect members' interests (there was the odd blip, notably the Maxwell scandal). Trust status was also the way companies could claim tax relief for their pension funds.

In fact, trust law is rather an old-fashioned way of going about business. At its heart is a small book that sets out the terms and conditions of the individual Trust. You are probably aware that somewhere in your files you have a copy of the "Principal" or "Consolidated" "Trust Deed" that describes the terms of your Trust. Typically a copy is given to each new trustee when they join the board. But because there have been so many changes in the industry a lot of boards have made numerous amendments to their Trust Deeds, so it is possible you have seen a copy of your Deed more recently.

Now, let's be honest. Have you ever actually read your Deed? Have you any idea what it actually says? Admit it, you have not. Perhaps you opened it briefly and saw the dense legalese and the endless sub-clauses that seem to go on for page after page.

Here is an example of typical off-putting jargon:

"Provided however that this clause shall not operate to preclude the Employers and the Trustees from making any specific amendments within their power under the Trust Deed to the said provisions of the old Trust Deed or otherwise under the Plan relating to such Members or any of them."

See what I mean? It's pretty intimidating stuff. I don't blame you for not reading it.

READING LESSONS

But think about it: you cannot be an effective trustee if you have not read the central document that defines your role and sets out how you must act in relation to the pension scheme. And you cannot represent your members if you do not know, for example, whether or not you can call an emergency meeting or whether the company can sack you and replace the entire board with a special trustee. That's precisely the kind of thing that is buried in all that legal jargon.

I'm going to labour this point in an attempt to drive it home. Read the Trust Deed from cover to cover.

Now read it again, skimming the jargon, but making sure you identify which bits actually say something. The document can be surprisingly revealing. For example, most trustees are shocked to find that the typical Deed clearly states that the sponsoring company can do pretty much anything it likes and the trustees are powerless to resist. Once you look carefully it becomes easier to spot the clauses and conditions that truly inform the governance of the Trust. They are often quite short clauses, because, unlike the legalese, they are making quite simple points – so many trustees can call a special meeting, the company can appoint X or Y, and so on.

Now read the document a third time. You should have a good sense of what matters by now. And once you have installed this into your brain, you should be able to attend meetings confident that you have the right foundations for discussing and taking decisions. Simple, really.

THE KEY POINTS

By definition, trustees only see their own Trust Deed – there is not much of a market in second-hand volumes. I confess that I have not seen more than a handful, and that does not qualify me as an expert reader. But there are some general pointers for all trustees, and I am grateful to Charles Cowling of Mercer Consulting for pointing these out. When Mr Cowling meets with a trustee board, the first thing he does is to take them through the Trust Deed and identify the key points. He looks for four things:

Investments – trustees will almost certainly have unilateral control over these. This means the trustees can likely use this power to drive the funding policy of the sponsor. And under the law, as we have already discussed, there is not much the sponsor can do about it. So, at one extreme, if you have control and want to make your fund less risky, you can buy annuities and force better funding of the remaining liabilities. Less extreme investment changes will also be likely to result in changes to the required contributions. The point is that unless you have read your Trust Deed, you won't know what you can do.

Contribution powers – who has the power to set contributions? This is a crucial factor and it varies widely. Sometimes it is trustees, sometimes the company, sometimes the actuary, and there are all sorts of different combinations. But as trustees, you can't be effective unless you know. The Trust Deed will tell you. If it is unclear, ask your lawyer for a ruling. You may well have greater power than you think.

Power of amendment and augmentation – again, this is crucial. Who gets to change the rules or alter, say, the level of benefits? This power relates directly to the issue of who gets to take the risk and who gets to keep any rewards from a risk-taking strategy.

Power to wind up – who has it and in what circumstances? Again, given the new legal landscape, this is a vital question and trustees must be able to answer it by reading their Trust Deed and understanding their powers. As we will see in more detail in Chapter Six, this is becoming a real issue for more and more trustees.

I hope that makes a little clearer why you should get your Trust Deed off the shelf now. That's if you know where it is...

THE POWER OF MINUTES

Another step towards becoming an effective trustee is to realise that you have to pay attention to some small things. The Trust Deed is one. Another is the minutes that are taken routinely at meetings, usually by a secretary to the Board of Trustees. When you became a trustee, were you given a set of minutes covering the past year's worth of meetings? If not then you should have been. And if you did get them, did you read them? Or did you, as most trustees do, turn up to your first meeting without having read them? You can get away with flying blind like that, but not if you want to be effective.

Why are the minutes so valuable? They will tell you what has been discussed, but more importantly they will give you clues as to who sits in which camp and who has the most to say. This depends, of course, on how the minutes are taken and the extent to which they identify individual trustees' participation in the meetings. Some minutes are more useful than others. However, even the worst minutes are full of information.

Minutes are the formal record of your deliberations. If there is a dispute in the future, the minutes will be the legal basis for any findings. So they are worth spending some time on. Normally they are circulated in draft form a few days after a trustee meeting. Most trustees think their job begins and ends in the meetings of the board, but that is quite wrong. You should read the draft minutes. It does not take long, but you might find that there is something wrongly recorded or misinterpreted. If you think it's hard being a trustee, imagine being the poor secretary. He or she is unlikely to have much grounding in pension matters, let alone in the jargon-prone field of actuarial assumptions and investments. So read the draft minutes and reply with corrections to anything you think is wrong or lacks precision.

PUT IT ON THE RECORD

If the minutes are the formal record of your proceedings, it follows that they form the only real way you can protect yourself against problems arising from the conduct of the board on which you sit. A real example might help to explain why you should focus on this apparently trivial matter.

A trustee of a major pension fund, which has almost £2 billion of assets but a whopping deficit as well, became aware that the trustee board was riddled with conflicts of interest and was not doing a great job of representing members' interests. He used all his skill to try to direct debate, but was mostly dismissed by the chairman of the board, who happened to be a former director of the company. So he tried a new tactic. When he raised a point or had an objection to a decision, he asked for his dissent to be minuted. This was not an easy thing to do. It meant raising his hand, calling for attention and saying something like "Mr Chairman, for the record could the minutes state specifically that I disagree with the decision the board has just taken." Or "Please, Mr Chairman, would the secretary note that I voted against the proposed asset allocation." But the policy was remarkably effective. By putting things on the record, the trustee made the rest of the board become more aware of the legal significance of what they were doing. He raised the stakes by making his fellow trustees a little uncomfortable. But he protected his own interests, and defended those of members, by doing so.

This story has an unhappy ending. After a few meetings, the trustee found that his requests for minutes were no longer resulting in the relevant references appearing in the actual minutes. Further, the chairman of the trustee board stopped circulating draft minutes, so there was no way for the trustee to make amendments and put the record straight. This made an awkward situation much worse. What could the trustee do next? He was reluctant to challenge the minutes when they were put up for approval at the next meeting (although this might have proved effective). He could have raised the issue under "AOB" as it is known – Any Other Business, that part of the trustee meeting when sundry matters not on the formal agenda are discussed. But that would be seen as even more aggressive than calling for minuted items in the first place. It would be a direct challenge to the chairman, who had plenty of support from the other trustees. Indeed, our trustee was already regarded as belonging to a one-man awkward squad. In the event it proved too stressful and the trustee resigned by not seeking a new term of office.

This is not meant to be a cautionary tale, although perhaps it reads rather like one. My intention is rather to show how powerful something apparently boring can be in practice. Minutes exist for a reason. Use them.

BACK TO RULES AND REGULATIONS

I mentioned above that there is a vital set of guidelines that were issued by the Pensions Regulator. These should not be confused with another document put out by the Regulator called imaginatively "Guidance from the Pensions Regulator". At the time of writing it consists of 60 pages of rather dry prose, but it's actually quite a useful summary of a trustee's duties and responsibilities (www.thepensionsregulator.gov.uk/trustees/guidance/index.aspx). The problem with it is that, as often happens with official guidance, it does not really convey what it is actually like to sit on a trustee board. Nor does it convey the flavour of the tensions and disputes that can arise. But you might find it helpful to print out a copy of the guidance.

Some of the points made by the Regulator must be understood by all trustees. First, trustees are subject to the law of the land as well as to trust law. Successive governments have tackled pensions. The Pensions Act of 1995 was designed to tighten up trust law in the wake of the Maxwell scandal. More relevant today is the Pensions Act of 2004. This introduced a lot of new rights and duties for trustees.

Perhaps the most important is that from April 2006 trustees are required by law to have "knowledge and understanding" of the law relating to pension schemes, their funding and the investment of their assets. This sounds rather formidable, and it's worth remembering my point that you cannot be expected to be an expert in everything. Some commentators have reacted to this stipulation by saying that trustees will have to sharpen up their act and greatly improve their knowledge. Perhaps. Indeed, you might argue that this is necessary regardless of the law if trustees want to be effective. But there are problems with the new law. "Knowledge" and "understanding" are subjective categories. No one can agree on exactly what they mean. Does knowledge, for example, mean a little or a lot?

Here is my advice. So long as you have a working knowledge and a sensible understanding of your role and make sure you ask your advisers when you don't know something, you will be acting prudently and lawfully. Interestingly, one of the new requirements is that trustees are familiar with the main documents that govern their pension scheme – including the Trust Deed. So it's not just me being boring when I urge you to read the Deed. You must.

ALL YOU NEED TO KNOW ABOUT BEING A PENSION FUND TRUSTEE

Chapter 4

LEARNING TO TAKE ADVICE

SPEED-READ SUMMARY

- Trustees rely on their advisers, especially their actuary

- Don't be afraid to challenge them and to question their ideas

- Complex calculations underlie actuarial advice, but their forecasts are inevitably wrong – the real issue is by how much

- Actuaries have been under fire for getting too much wrong, including assumptions about longevity

- A "new school" of actuaries has challenged conventional thinking about advice to pension funds, especially attacking the "cult of equity" and applying a mark-to-market approach

- £100 of equities is worth the same as £100 of bonds

- The actuarial valuation is one of the most important exercises for trustees to commission and understand

- Your actuary sets the discount rate, so you should challenge this key assumption

Remember in Chapter One I listed all of the people who sit around the table at a typical meeting of a trustee board. Put aside for a moment the company representatives who are often present – they usually do not contribute much, especially as they typically are drawn from the company's finance department, so will naturally defer to the finance director who just happens to be sitting there as a trustee. What about the others? In order of importance they are:

- Your actuary
- Your consultant(s) – they often travel in pairs, one senior, the other junior
- Your scheme administrator
- Your lawyer

Less often in attendance, but essential by law, is your scheme auditor, who prepares a statement about the contributions payable to the scheme and conducts an annual audit of the scheme's accounts.

You should also have occasional visits from your fund managers, so that they can report on progress and answer any questions you might have about how the assets are performing under their care. These parts of the meeting are often fairly tedious. (Indeed, on some boards trustees have been more concerned with gleaning investment tips for their own use than in grilling the fund manager!) If the performance is satisfactory, then the appearance is a bit of a courtesy call on the fund manager's part. If performance has been poor, then there might be fireworks, but more often there is muted embarrassment on both sides. I will come back to this problem when I discuss investment and managing your assets in Chapters Six and Seven. Just occasionally it is necessary to fire your fund manager, but you have to pick your moment carefully!

This chapter explains what your most important adviser – your actuary – does. The next chapter looks in detail at your other main adviser – your pension and/or investment consultants – explaining what they do in practice and when and why you should listen to them. Administrators and lawyers are dealt with rather briefly at the start of Chapter Five.

AN END TO DEFERENCE

But first some general remarks. I think it is important that you should take care not to be too deferential to advisers. The relationship is a tricky one. After all, as I have argued, you cannot be expected to be an expert on everything, and the law encourages you to rely on expert advice before you make decisions. So it seems natural that you should turn to those experts and generally defer to their suggestions. Yes, in theory.

But there are some major caveats to this position. In practice, advice is only as good as the money that buys it. The bigger your fund, the more likely it is that you can tap into really good advice, especially when it comes to the vital area of investment decisions. But if you are a smallish fund, the chances are that you will not be getting a visit from the top star at your firm of actuaries or consultants. I know of one fund where the trustees realised after a year or so that they actually knew more than the junior consultant sent along to "advise" them. And I know of plenty of funds where the advice offered has been timid, misguided or just plain wrong. As we will see, advisers can be as blinkered sometimes as their clients.

In other words, you should not be afraid to challenge your advisers. Don't just accept what they say at face value. Often, if you ask a pertinent question, you can uncover gaps in their knowledge. Sometimes you will find situations when it seems they are less concerned to give you good advice than they are to keep relations smooth all round. I'm not suggesting you should be cynical. But you should definitely be sceptical.

Advisers are like any group of paid professionals. They try to avoid conflict wherever possible because conflict gives the impression that they are somehow failing in their job. They like to appear competent and well informed, so do not like being caught out. They travel as a pack, generally giving the same advice to all of their clients and only changing that advice when they think it is time to back the next horse. (This, of course, is a cardinal sin because it falls into the trap of thinking that all pension funds are the same.) If they realise that you have a point, they like to present it as if that had been their idea or intention all along. And they are used to baffling people with terms such as stochastic analysis and multi-scenario regressions when all else has failed.

BAFFLED BY GOBBLEDYGOOK

This last point is extremely important. If you have been a trustee for a while, you will be familiar with the thick volumes of analysis and prognostication that is the standard fare of actuaries and consultants. Another of trustees' little secrets is that very few actually bother to read these volumes beyond a quick scan of the executive summary. They are boring and intimidating, especially to non-mathematicians. And how are you going to cope with a statistical regression analysis if you gave up maths at school forty years ago?

Well, you can cope, and the way forward is to do what I suggested you must do in order to get to know your Trust Deed. Reading papers, even if it takes a full day or more of preparation before a meeting, is the only way to arm yourself to have a meaningful discussion with your advisers. And it is absolutely the only way to tease out any chinks in your advisers' armour and, trust me, there will be chinks.

I suggest below some questions you should ask of your advisers. In Chapters Seven and Eight I will explain why this is especially important when it comes to making investment decisions. But the big point is that asking questions, including tough ones, of your advisers is part of your duties as a trustee. It is legally safe to rely on their advice. But if you rely on it totally and never question it, then you are not being an effective trustee.

The Pensions Regulator has some sensible things to say about advisers. He says simply that trustees should make sure they understand what help and advice they can expect from the different advisers. Make sure you know the limits of their advice. This includes asking them, for example, when you should seek further expert advice. And although trustees are allowed to delegate duties to "suitably qualified people", they still have the overall responsibility for any actions taken. It's important to remember that. Your advisers often assume positions that imply they have greater knowledge than you (and so, in many cases, they should), so you will have a natural tendency to defer to them. But you must never lose sight of the fact that the buck stops with you. So if you do delegate something, make sure you have a procedure for checking that the job is being done properly. In the case of scheme administration, which a lot of funds have outsourced to specialists, this might be an annual or semi-annual audit. If it is something more fundamental, the monitoring might be more regular and intrusive.

THE "SCIENCE" OF THE ACTUARY

What are actuaries and are they really boring? The profession certainly has a staid image. Here is a small selection from the enormous number of available jokes about actuaries – they are much like "dumb blonde" or "how many XXs does it take to change a lightbulb?" jokes, but they give a flavour of actuaries' reputation.

- Actuary: "There are three kinds of actuaries. Those that can count. And those that can't."
- An actuary is someone who wanted to be an accountant, but didn't have the personality for it.
- An accountant is someone who wanted to be an actuary, but didn't have the personality for it.
- Two people are flying in a hot air balloon and realise they are lost. They see a man on the ground, so they navigate the balloon to where they can speak to him. They yell to him, "Can you help us – we're lost." The man on the ground replies, "You're in a hot air balloon, about 200 feet off the ground." One of the people in the balloon replies to the man on the ground, "You must be an actuary. You gave us information that is accurate, but completely useless." The actuary on the ground yells to the people in the balloon, "You must be in marketing." They yell back, "Yes, how did you know?" The actuary says, "Well, you're in the same situation you were in before you talked to me, but now it's my fault."
- Definition of a computer: an actuary with a heart.
- What is the difference between an introverted actuary and an extroverted actuary? An introverted actuary stares at his own feet during a conversation, while an extroverted one stares at the other person's feet.
- An actuary is standing with a farmer looking at two fields of sheep. The farmer asks how many sheep there are in the two

fields. The actuary looks at them and says "1,007". Farmer: "How on earth did you get that figure?", Actuary: "Well, there are 7 in that field, and about a thousand in the other one".

But what do actuaries do? They famously calculate longevity tables (that is, work out how long people will live on average), and for decades have used a certain mystique to protect themselves from outside scrutiny. Access to the profession is controlled by the Institute of Actuaries and the Faculty of Actuaries, which make sure that training is long and boring. But once they qualify actuaries are well paid and they have sewn up a market for advice to pension funds and insurance companies, which depend on long-term projections as the basis for decisions. As one actuary put it to me, "We are the ultimate closed shop!"

Think about a pension fund. The standard view is that it has long-term goals – mainly to meet its obligations to retirees far into the future by ensuring that it has adequate funding today and for the foreseeable future. A less standard, but arguably more helpful view, is that a pension fund is a safety net for its members, and that its financial needs can be modelled with reasonable accuracy in the short term, but with decreasing accuracy as forecasts move further into the future (not unlike a weather forecast). Some actuaries are refreshingly honest about their inability to forecast. Others are stuck in the mindset of a couple of decades ago, when actuaries enjoyed an unhealthy mystique and were almost never challenged.

Anyway, back to the intellectual challenge. A fund's obligations/liabilities are tricky to model. You don't know today exactly how much, and when, you will be required to pay out in the future. But the key word is "exactly". You know within certain bounds, because you know how many employees you have, how many deferred members and how many current retirees. And you know roughly how much has been promised to date in the form of accrued benefits. That means you can model a "no-risk" portfolio – one that holds assets whose cashflows match the cashflows required to meet the promises. You can also project into the future how many more benefits are likely to accrue, based on assumptions about future service (that is, work!) and how fast salaries are likely to rise (remember, pensions are deferred pay!). You must take into account future inflation, which can have big effects on the value of liabilities and assets, as well as on salaries. Finally, thanks to actuaries, you know how long your retirees are likely to live, from which you can derive a long-term horizon for your obligations.

A point here for trustees: one way to picture your job is to think in terms of those cashflows that the actuary is modelling. Are you confident that you will have enough money in future to meet those cashflows? How confident?

MAKING MODELS

Let's stop here for a moment. It should be obvious that modelling all of this is indeed quite a challenge. You need a lot of information before you can even begin to tackle the question of long-term liabilities. And you need some mathematical sophistication to handle the several variables that go into your calculations. Even if you can handle all of this, it is only the first stage of the bigger process, which includes deciding on the basis of the liabilities how you should fund your pension scheme and how you should deploy its assets.

Pension schemes have essentially outsourced this function to actuaries. Given the complexity of the task, that is fair enough.

Before I explain some of the intellectual thinking behind the actuarial approach to managing pension funds, it might help to list briefly what you can expect from your actuary. (I have adapted this list from the Pensions Regulator's guidance in an attempt to make it more practical.) Start from the observation that the actuary is there to advise you on "all aspects of the funding" of your scheme. This has several elements:

- What do you need to meet the minimum funding required by law?
- Every three years, or more often depending on the circumstances of the fund, a full actuarial valuation is needed to value the scheme's liabilities, so that these can be compared to the scheme's assets and a determination made whether the fund is in surplus or deficit.
- Allowing for this, what contributions are appropriate and over what timeframe?

- What kind of investments are suitable for meeting the scheme's liabilities in future?
- What is the right way to calculate how much you should give to people who transfer their assets out of the fund, or who want to bring in assets from another fund? (Note – the latter has become a rare circumstance because few individuals want to transfer assets into a fund that is in deficit and might be shut down.)
- Are there any special circumstances or events that might affect the fund's viability or challenge the assumptions on which it is being run?

As you can see, even this is a pretty hefty list. So it might be helpful to offer the ultimate summary, as suggested by Cliff Speed. Trustees need to address two central questions:

1. Do we have enough money to meet the promises made so far?
2. How much cash do we need for the new promises made this year?

If you can keep those in mind, you will not go far wrong.

But back to actuaries. You should be able to see (and know from your own experience) that an actuary can be in a tricky position. Often he is working for the scheme advising the trustees, but is also working for the sponsoring company, advising them on financial assumptions, discussing/negotiating on contribution levels, and, these days, talking with the sponsor about how to eliminate big deficits. This is a raging conflict of interest and I will come back to it in later chapters.

To be fair, it is also something that actuaries are acutely aware of. There is an entire section on conflicts of interest in the Professional Conduct Standards issued by the Institute of Actuaries, and Paragraph 5.1 specifically says that actuaries should give advice to their client that is unaffected by the interests of another party.

A MIXED PERFORMANCE

But trickiness aside, have actuaries done a good job? It depends. They have plenty of critics today, not least from within the ranks of their own profession. Where were they when funds en masse were taking big bets on equities, while their sponsors took contribution holidays? Why were they remarkably slow to recognise that they faced a potential conflict of interest if they tried to serve trustee boards while simultaneously advising companies? And why were they even slower to produce longevity tables that reflected the growing propensity for retirees to have thirty or forty years of retirement rather than ten or twenty? All this by way of saying that their record is far from unblemished.

To be scrupulously fair, of course there were some actuaries who spoke out quite loudly over the issues in the above paragraph. My point is that the profession as a whole preferred to keep its head in the sand.

In fact, so blemished was its reputation that in the wake of the Equitable Life debacle, the Government asked Sir Derek Morris to conduct a thorough review of the actuarial profession. One of his wittier observations was to point out that the profession's motto is "Certainty out of uncertainties", which, if you think about it, instantly fails the truth-in-advertising test. (Sir Derek might have been paraphrasing: the Institute of Actuaries' notepaper has a different motto that reads "Making financial sense of the future".)

Everybody knows that in the future there is an enormous range of possible outcomes. Yet the profession has lulled trustees (and perhaps itself) by typically presenting only three alternative futures, two of which are usually extremes. Sir Derek castigated actuaries for avoiding or resisting a clear presentation of the risks "inherent in an assessment of an uncertain future".

The actuarial profession has, however, been reforming itself, notably by engaging in a fierce debate about its methods and intellectual framework. You might remember that in Chapter Two I referred to the "new school" of actuarial thinking. This was born in 1997 when a group of young-ish actuaries, led by Jon Exley, Shyam Mehta and Andrew Smith, broke ranks and questioned the way they and their colleagues had been doing their jobs. At the centre of their argument was the proper advice for actuaries to give pension funds and the proper way to account for the riskiness of pension fund assets.

This debate is vitally important for trustees. The way the new actuaries think about pension funds and their liabilities is directly linked to new ways of managing funds. For example, most of you will have heard of the decision by the trustees of Boots plc to move their fund's assets entirely into bonds (a move that has since been watered down by a new set of trustees). That decision rested entirely on the insights of the new actuaries, as well as on the courage and perseverance of John Ralfe, then the head of corporate finance of Boots and a rare example of someone who successfully negotiated the interests of the fund's members and the sponsoring company. Some other big companies have done the same, but have sought no publicity for their move.

If you do not understand the basic thinking behind the new school, then you will struggle to be an effective trustee. So I need to spell it out in some detail. Don't worry. I'm not going to get too technical. Remember what I argued about your inability to be an expert in everything? You should not aspire to turn yourself into a leading financial economist just because actuaries are having a spat about what they believe and therefore what advice they give to trustees. You do not need to start arguing with your actuary about the principles of mean variance analysis.

Rather I'm going to try to explain the actuarial debate in terms you should have no trouble understanding. This, by the way, is quite a challenge in itself. Obviously there is a danger I will oversimplify and miss important subtleties in the arguments. To minimise the risk of this I will also list references to some of the original papers that have set out the case for changing the way actuaries advise pension funds. The key paper – the one that sent a shockwave through the industry thanks to its rigour and insight – was presented in 1997 at the Institute of Actuaries. If you want to, then you should read this and other papers for yourself – they are demanding, but very rewarding if you find that sort of thing interesting. But you should not need to.

Instead, you should be able to ask your actuary to explain the debate to you and to justify his advice in light of the new thinking. (Just as you should ask your actuary whether he is comfortable also representing the sponsoring company. Go on, see what they say!)

WHERE IT ALL BEGAN

A useful starting point is to set out very briefly the status quo ante bellum: in Chapter Two I described the problem of pension fund deficits and how these came about. One major reason was that almost all funds were significantly exposed to equities. It was not uncommon for a fund to have 90% or even 95% of its assets in the stockmarket. This had seemed like a perfectly sensible thing to do when share prices were rising strongly. But once markets tumbled, it quickly seemed like a disaster, as fund after fund plunged into deficit. (Interestingly, despite this, you will still find plenty of trustees and company representatives who think equities are the natural asset class for pension funds – I will discuss this in subsequent chapters.)

Think for a minute what this meant. Most funds were almost entirely exposed to equities, and mostly UK equities at that – funds' exposure to the biggest UK company by market capitalisation was often greater than their entire US exposure. They almost entirely ignored other asset classes – bonds, property, private equity and so on.

Why? Put aside investment arguments, because these were not much in evidence. If you ask people who were trustees in the 1980s and early 1990s, they will tell you that there was very little discussion during meetings about the logic of holding equities. It was simply the done thing. Indeed, I spoke to one trustee who said it was considered a radical idea at the time to argue that a scheme should hold its equities passively in an index fund rather than give the money to an active manager who would charge higher fees and normally fail to outperform the market. (If I lost you in that sentence, don't worry, all will become clear in the chapters on investment below.)

But there is another reason funds were overwhelmingly invested in equities: their advisers told them it was fine. Almost the entire actuarial profession went along with companies and trustees who put all of their eggs into the equities basket. In fact, given their reputation for prudence and conservatism, actuaries did something even more extraordinary than that. They presumed that the strong performance of shares would go on in the future with such certainty that it was actually less risky for a fund to own them than it was for it to hold bonds. They were erroneously taught by their Institute that equities matched salary-related liabilities (they don't and never have, by the way). No prizes for guessing who wrote: "The howler is so self-evident that mere technical incompetence cannot explain it away. We can see the presence of at least two of the deadly sins: sloth and greed. Clients bought this palpable untruth because it suited them to do so." Yes, it was PwC's John Shuttleworth. But Martin Taylor, former chairman of WH Smith and also former boss of Barclays Bank, is equally damning – see below for his version of the same point.

Let's go further with the logic of this, because it will make it much easier to understand where the new actuaries are coming from. If equities are seen as less risky than bonds or other assets, then it follows that the more equities a fund holds the less risky it becomes. So, said the old actuaries (with, it must be said, strong support from both companies and the accounting profession), an equity-rich fund that would have strong returns in future needed less funding today than a different fund that held less exciting assets.

As you will see later on, this produced an accounting nonsense that has had profound effects on the entire pension fund industry. But it also meant that companies actively wanted their funds to hold lots of equities. That way they would pay lower contributions, something that always pleases shareholders and managers, who can put the cash to other uses. You only have to think about my earlier discussion of trustees' relationships with their companies to see that there was never going to be much resistance from trustee boards.

In case you think I might be labouring this point, this is a good place at which to put into numbers what actuaries' wonderful assumptions have meant in practice for trustees. I have taken this example because it seems to me to typify the kinds of problems that trustees have faced. I'm quoting from an actuarial review that was undertaken for a medium-sized fund in 2004. The actuary gave his report to the trustee board in April that year. And towards the front of the report (there was no convenient summary or totting up of the key numbers) was a page headed "Portfolio Analysis: change over the period". And here is how the page read:

"The overall plan deficit at December 31st 2003 has come about thanks to various factors that have affected the plan since the last triennial review. The changes are summarised in the table below:

	£000s
Excess liabilities at December 31st 2000:	**15,790**
Interest on deficit at Dec 31st 2000	4,756
Lower than expected returns on plan assets	65,477
Higher than expected contributions	(7,924)
Higher than expected increases in earnings	2,545
Lower than expected increases in pensions payable	(1,232)
Withdrawals from active membership	(1,115)
Changes in assumptions	(14,003)
Miscellaneous	(756)
Deficit at December 31st 2003	**63,538** "

Does anything strike you about this? I think it is quite striking. You might ask whether the actuary actually got anything right at the previous valuation, given that there are so many factors that seem to have altered. Surely they weren't all unexpected? But then, look again at the list of factors. It's a useful and rather stunning reminder that in a world of forecasting, the test is not whether you were right or wrong, but by how much you were right or wrong. As when you read any set of numbers or accounts, it's always a good idea to look at the big figures, the ones that make a difference. And in this case there is one startling number – the £65 million of returns that simply went missing in the brief three-year period between valuations. If nothing else illustrates the effects of the cult of equity, then this surely does. Over the period the deficit went from small-ish and manageable to become a major headache.

But the above should trigger a broader thought. Just look at how many assumptions have gone into the calculation, and then count up how many have been utterly wrong. Note also that but for the adoption of a new set of assumptions, which allowed £14 million to be shaved off the problem, the fund's deficit would have been even greater. Even "Miscellaneous" hides three quarters of a million pounds of adjustment. How many trustees ever stop to ask what exactly that consists of? It can't be lunches that the actuary has decided to forego. Actually, in this example, Miscellaneous is actually quite a small number given that it normally includes a bunch of the actuary's assumptions about such matters as early retirement rates, commutation values, mortality rates, lump sums and so on. In many accounts, the inevitably incorrect forecasts can add up to a much bigger number.

THE CULT OF EQUITY

How did the new actuaries attack the status quo? They applied finance theory to make a blindingly obvious point. What is something worth? In financial markets, something is worth only what the market will pay for it. If you have £100 of equities and £100 of bonds and you can sell them for face value, then they are worth exactly the same. The market does not give you £110 for the £100-worth equities – why should it? Aha, an old actuary might say, it should because equities are expected to produce higher returns in future than bonds, so they should be worth more today.

That is, of course, rubbish. No serious economist would give it so much as the time of day. There is a reason equities are expected to produce higher future returns than bonds – they are riskier and are almost equally likely to produce lower returns, or even negative returns to the point that their owner is wiped out. To pile on the clichés, there is no free lunch. This is especially true for long-term investors such as pension funds. The longer you hold equities, the worse the potentially bad outcomes become. As John Shuttleworth once pointed out, it's the same risk as if you tossed a coin again and again betting on heads, only for tails to keep on coming up – you dig yourself ever deeper into losses. Equities pay more because they are riskier. But that does not alter the fact that £100 worth of shares is still worth £100. Even the best-meant advice of the top actuary from the leading firm of Drone, Ledger & Snooze cannot alter that fact.

This exposes the central fallacy of traditional pension fund management, whether by trustees on their own or advised by actuaries who should know better. The scary thing is that there are still plenty of trustees today who believe that equities are worth more than bonds and are prepared to load their portfolio towards them. They cannot see beyond the fog in which they have run their fund. And it is relatively recent for actuaries to have tried themselves to blow away some of that fog.

It is tempting to think that something obviously flawed does not need a serious rebuttal. Tempting, but a mistake. It cannot be stated too often just how mistaken the traditional approach has been. Arguably it only persisted because stockmarkets were in a two-decade-long secular bull market. If equities had behaved normally during that time (they tried to by crashing in 1987), the myth of "stocks for the long run" might never have been peddled, let alone bought with other people's money.

But even after the puncturing of the equity myth, some actuaries persisted with a perverse logic. Take this example, from another medium-sized fund. As recently as March 2004 its actuary was writing the following:

"If the assets were to be invested in the lowest risk assets, ie, gilts, then the [actuarial] valuation should assume that the returns to be generated from the assets are also relatively low. This gives a weak funding position and a high contribution rate required from the employer to fund the benefits. Alternatively, if the Trustees continue to invest in high risk assets, such as equities, then it is reasonable for the actuary to assume that higher returns will be generated from these assets than from gilts over the long term. This can reduce the contribution rate required from the employer in order to fund the benefits. The degree to which it is appropriate to take account of expected equity outperformance in setting the basis and hence the contribution rate, is a matter for the actuary to use his judgement [sic] in consultation with the Trustees and company."

As I was writing this out I came across several phrases I wanted to put into italics to give them emphasis. But then I realised that the whole passage neatly sums up the actuarial problem I have been describing. In the ugly prose there is a newfound recognition that equities are riskier than other assets. But there is also a blithe assumption that this does not really translate into a riskier profile for the fund, because, of course, the very reasonable actuary also must take into account the appetite of the company to pay contributions and these will be lower if the equity allocation is higher. Note, too, the subtle presentation of the actuary as ultimate and god-like arbiter. The final sentence basically says to trustees "Don't worry your heads too much about this, it's ultimately my judgment that counts."

HOW MUCH RISK, EXACTLY?

New actuaries made a further observation on the risk question. How much risk should trustees be prepared to take and what should be the proper basis for actuarial advice on this? In the early 1990s, 1992 to be exact, a paper by Paul Thornton and AF Wilson that was to become extremely influential was presented in the journal of the Institute of Actuaries. It was called "A realistic approach to pension funding" and it contained a remarkable assertion: a risk could be viewed as prudent if it had a 60% chance of a successful outcome. A subsequent commentator remarked that most members of pension schemes would be pretty shocked if you told them that there was only a 70% chance that their benefits would be secure. But it took until 2004, when Charles Cowling, Tim Gordon and Cliff Speed presented another paper to the Institute of Actuaries for the Thornton and Wilson approach to be debunked. Messrs Cowling, Gordon and Speed argued that the proper approach to "Funding Defined Benefit Pension Schemes" was to relate funding targets clearly and straightforwardly to the solvency of the scheme. Forget 60% or even 70% chance. Funds needed to think more about an insurance model than one of largely unfettered risk-taking.

This view has been gradually permeating the actuarial profession, but it has not yet become orthodoxy. However, it has successfully changed the debate and made actuaries far more aware of their responsibility when it comes to this aspect of their advice. The issue remains what actuaries do when they leave their offices and sit down with their clients. What line do they take when it comes to giving real professional advice?

Indeed, the new actuaries noted the extraordinary irony that actuaries, famous for their conservatism, had collectively embraced a set of ideas that were so risky that they amounted to playing fast and loose with pension fund assets. Not only did they accept a crazy assumption that equity prices move in a straight line, they also systematically and severely underpriced funds' liabilities. They went so far that they helped to make pension funds more exciting and venturesome than hedge funds. So the new actuaries also attacked from a second flank – that of pension funds' liabilities.

NEW THINKING ON LIABILITIES

The £100 equity/bond point is pretty clear. The "second front" relates to another lesson derived from finance theory. And that relates in turn directly to actuarial practice. Let's go back to the financial legerdemain I mentioned above by which funds that held lots of equities were deemed to require lower contributions today on the grounds that equities have higher expected returns than other assets. The clear implication was that somehow the high proportion of equities had magically reduced the fund's liabilities – otherwise you could not justify reducing contributions. Comforting for trustees, that, but completely wrong. The liabilities do not change, regardless of what assets the fund holds. They are simply unaffected.

This makes sense if you think about it. I can hold portfolio X or Y, but neither affects my liabilities of Z, because Z is an independent variable calculated by looking at long-term future cashflows. When you apply a calculation to work out a contribution rate that will meet the future liabilities, you can make it higher or lower and you can throw in all kinds of assumptions, but you do not alter the liabilities by one penny. They are what they are, regardless of how you try to meet them.

New actuaries had a neat way of explaining this. Imagine, they said, you borrow £1,000 from the bank. Obviously you have an obligation to pay it back (ie, a liability). Suppose you decided to invest the £1,000 in the stockmarket. Do you think that decision means you no longer owe £1,000? Of course not. And to drive the point home, what would the bank manager say if you suggested that because of your investment you should be able to make smaller repayments on the loan? Most bank managers would call back the loan immediately on the grounds that you were mad. Yet an "old actuary" manager would happily accept such a deal and the consequence that you no longer owed £1,000. Put like this, it's a pretty topsy-turvy approach to running a pension fund.

Martin Taylor, chairman of the trustee board of WH Smith, produced a similarly colourful description of the old actuarial approach to liabilities: the "convention according to which the composition of the assets determines the size of the liabilities is one of the weirdest emanations of the human mind. It's a metaphor – like saying that the advent of jet planes made the Atlantic narrower – and metaphor has a limited place in finance."

For a minority of trustees this will be so obvious that they might be insulted to read this chapter. Surely every self-respecting trustee knows this? Not so. It's actually quite complicated for a non-professional to grasp the importance of this seemingly arcane theory. And some professionals have not yet caught up with reality. If you don't believe me, try asking your actuary two questions at your next meeting. Ask him privately, if you like, before the formal proceedings begin. Here are the questions:

Question One: "Do you think £100 of equities is worth the same as £100 of bonds?"

Question Two: "Does the value of our liabilities depend on what kind of assets we invest in?"

If I am right, you will get some peculiar, contorted and possibly wrong answers!

OLD THINKING ON LIABILITIES

It's worth pointing out that over the last couple of decades there has been a very important change in how liabilities are viewed. As Charles Cowling has pointed out, two decades ago solvency was simply not an issue for pension funds – on that measure, many funds were 200–300% solvent (hard to believe, but true). So liabilities were seen as largely "aspirational": that is to say the sponsor and the trustees, with help from actuaries, would address together the question of how much surplus they wished to make so that it could be divided up. And they would set funding accordingly. In that context, it was not completely mad to make some assumptions about investment returns and hence to favour equities.

Since then, however, the view on liabilities has moved towards seeing them as inherently fixed/guaranteed. In that framework, the old approach is quite inappropriate, but companies have been quite slow to realise the true costs of the guarantees they have written to their workers. Indeed, the entire pensions industry has been slow to grasp this.

Now, to some extent I am getting ahead of myself here. Some of this discussion probably belongs in the chapters below that focus on investment. These insights based on finance theory obviously have big implications for how you manage a fund's assets. But I have laid them out here because I believe it is impossible to make effective use of your actuary unless you understand the background to today's arguments about both liabilities and assets. If you understand the pages above, then you should have sufficient tools to ask meaningful questions of your actuary, where once you could only nod as they in effect told you what you had to do.

A little bit of history explains another apparent nonsense that is otherwise inexplicable. Where did the idea come from that it was acceptable and sensible to spread the paying off of deficits over many years? The answer is that it came from an accounting convention that was originally introduced to smooth the handling of surpluses – SSAP24. This famous standard spread surpluses over the average future working lifetime. So when surpluses became deficits, the idea of spreading them for accounting purposes was already an accepted one. Only fairly recently has a new approach been seen as both sensible and desirable. For trustees, this is a boon – you can get your money back much sooner, rather than wait more than a decade for it to be grudgingly handed over.

ACTUARIAL ASIDES

If you have been a trustee for a while, then chances are you have been through a "full actuarial valuation". This process happens every three years by law, and sounds terribly grand. Actually, I think it's a way for actuaries to charge you more than they should for something that should be quite routine given that it's their job to make complex calculations. It probably costs more for the fund to track down and provide the required numbers than it does for the actuary to crunch them. (That said, I accept the point made by one reader who happens to be an actuary. He observed that actuaries are good value for money compared to fund managers, who charge far more for their services.)

The valuation is a necessary and useful exercise. Without it you would never know whether the fund is in good health or in need of an injection. But it has limitations and it is important you understand these. In a typical set of company accounts there is always a profit and loss account and a balance sheet. The former describes what happened to the business during the reporting period. The latter gives a snapshot of the business's financial position on a given date. On a basic accounting course, you will always be reminded that by the time the balance sheet has been reported it is no longer accurate – by the nature of things, a snapshot taken one day is inaccurate the next week, even less so after a month and not very useful six months later. The same is true for actuarial valuations.

Let me try to sum up why this can cause frustrations. Imagine you are sitting in a meeting where the actuary makes a lovely presentation about the complicated valuation process, all illustrated by a handy set of slides and print-outs. And ultimately what he describes is the state of the fund on a given date, let's say March 31. That means our trustee meeting is probably in early July because the actuary has needed time to prepare his complex analysis. For the sake of illustration, imagine the actuary says that the fund is in deficit by £60m and that something must be done to increase the company's contribution rate.

How useful is this information? Well, it's quite useful in a broad-brush sort of way. But imagine that the next item on the agenda is a report from your consultants on investment performance over the previous quarter, the period from April 1 to the end of June. (Unlike actuaries, investment managers should have no trouble reporting their performance in a matter of days.) According to these figures, there was an unexpectedly nice £10 million rise in the assets over the period thanks to a jump in bond prices. Surely that means you can adjust the actuary's deficit downwards by £10 million, so there is less need to ask for higher contributions?
Wrong. Just as investment performance has moved on, so has the

fund overall, including the liabilities because they depend on how much bonds cost too. The snapshot from March is no longer accurate.

In other words, trying to assess the true position of the fund is like trying to hit a moving target. It is almost impossible to have a fixed view of the state of affairs.

Because so many funds are in deficit and require more maintenance than they would if they were healthier, actuaries have had to become more flexible on valuations. Trustees have been asking more often for a rough-and-ready valuation to support their decision-making. You can see why. If they are thinking of approaching the sponsoring company to ask for a cash injection, for example, or simply trying to wrap their heads around how bad things really are, then they need to present a meaningful number as part of the process. Otherwise they risk being ridiculed by the company for misrepresenting the true state of things.

This means as trustees you might be spending more money than you know. You need to make sure you ask your actuary how much it costs each time you ask for an update. Be aggressive – it is not that tricky for the actuary to produce what you need, especially if the sponsoring company is willing to provide the necessary information (which it should be).

A MOVING TARGET

It might be helpful for me to give another example of the 'moving target' problem. It relates to another discussion that you will have with your actuary and a document you will be asked to sign. Once all the calculations have been done, the actuary works out the level of contribution that will be required to fund the pension plan adequately. This used to be something that involved the trustees only tangentially – it was left largely between the actuary and the company to agree a number that both parties could live with. These days, however, the trustees have much more power (as we will see in more detail below) and actuaries are obliged to include them more in discussions and even accede to their demands.

I made the point above that trustees are dealing with several unforeseen consequences of the decision to close defined-benefit schemes to new members, one of which is that a faster fall in the number of active members has damaged funds' demographics. In many cases this has meant that it is no longer appropriate to fund the scheme on a percentage of "pensionable salary" basis – there just aren't enough active members to produce sufficient contributions that way. Actuaries have responded by reducing the weight of pensionable salaries in their funding formula and introducing a fixed element to contributions. So a "Schedule of Contributions" (this is the document you will be asked to sign) often now has a variable salaries element and a fixed monthly amount calculated by the actuary and agreed to by the company. An overall contribution rate is derived by adding the two together. If that sounds straightforward, then ask yourself whether it allows you to project ahead how the fund will look in a year's time. Assuming you know the required funding level, surely you can see whether or not a proposed schedule of contributions is adequate?

I don't think you can, for two reasons. One is that what was once considered adequate is no longer acceptable. Before the Pensions Regulator got into his stride and before the law began to change to reflect funds' poor health, actuaries thought it quite reasonable to view the process of closing a deficit over, say, ten or 12 or even 20 years. And they thought this even if there were good grounds for questioning the strength of the sponsor's covenant or doubting its long-term financial health.

Now that has changed. Remember that trustees are expected to behave more like bankers. So ask yourself this: would a bank lend on these terms? At no interest? Of course not. Such a long time horizon is no longer considered prudent and trustees are expected to be far more aggressive in seeking early payments that will reduce deficits as quickly as possible. So actuaries have had to follow suit and become more aggressive with sponsors. That means asking them for a lot more money, in the form of either lump sums or increased contributions that will pay down the deficit faster. (It also means questioning how much risk should be taken with the assets, but that is another matter and is discussed in Chapter Seven below.) This has made it difficult for trustees, who have to sign pieces of paper that give a snapshot of one moment's decision on contributions knowing that the view tomorrow might be utterly different, depending on how effectively they, and their actuary, negotiate with the company.

The second reason is that companies are not stupid. Many of them now realise that it is extremely inefficient to have a deficit in their pension fund. It saddles them with time-consuming administration and hampers their ability to manoeuvre. So more and more companies are beginning to suggest themselves that they should throw a slug of money at their deficit, either to reduce it substantially or to reduce it sufficiently that the heat goes out of negotiations with the trustees and actuary (this is quite separate from the more worrying issue of whether the company is also considering capping accrued benefits, of which more later). It should be a routine matter by now for trustees to ask for dialogue with the company on the question of giving a lump sum to the fund that will have a meaningful impact on the deficit. And that is fine, but it also means that until such a sum is forthcoming trustees do not know whether their current level of funding is prudent or whether they should be demanding a much higher level of contributions. I hope you can see that you are facing, in effect, a moving target.

NEW THINKING ABOUT LONGEVITY

It has been pretty difficult to miss the controversy over longevity, and there is little point in going over it in detail in this book. However, there is a possible "longevity trap" that some funds might fall into, and this is worth discussing briefly so that as a trustee you can ask the right questions of your actuary. The simple fact is that observers, including actuaries for whom it is a vital variable, seem to have systematically underestimated a sustained increase in longevity in the population as a whole. This has been horrid for pension funds, which face the prospect that their retirees will live far longer than was anticipated, drawing pensions that it was assumed would have ceased much earlier. Some funds have had a "longevity shock" when faced with the new projections.

So should funds face the new reality and simply adopt new

mortality tables that were published late in 2005? In a word, no. Before they do that, they need to address the longevity issue in a little more detail. As Charles Cowling rightly points out, mortality and longevity is a "non-trivial" matter: it is very difficult to make sense of the data that are presented in even the most up-to-date tables. For one thing, within the overall numbers there can be very wide variations that make generalising a dangerous thing. People in Glasgow might even have lower life expectancy than they did a decade or two ago, while people in Devon are living much longer. So what is a sensible mortality assumption for a pension fund? It depends. People in retirement schemes have longer life expectations than the population in general, but there are even differences between schemes. For instance, white-collar schemes might have quite different mortality from blue-collar ones.

The biggest unknown, says Mr Cowling, is what rate of improvement in longevity should be built into actuarial models of the future. Remember that this is one of the critical assumptions in a valuation. So should the recent rate of increase in life expectancy be extrapolated into the future? Probably not, because it has been so fast as to be potentially unsustainable. Think of fears over rising levels of obesity, and you have one good reason why the rate of increase might already have begun to tail off.

This is just to scratch the surface of a hugely complex issue. But it ought to be sufficient for trustees to realise that they need to talk to their actuary about this before they blithely accept a new set of assumptions.

An aside: greater longevity does not matter as much for pension funds if real interest rates are high. The problem is that at the moment real interest rates are historically low.

It is also worth noting that quoted companies are beginning to disclose their mortality assumptions as part of a general increase in the amount of information they are providing to investors about their pension schemes. In 2004, Rio Tinto said that its mortality tables implied that a 60-year-old man has a life expectancy of 24 years. Hanson reported that a 65-year-old male pensioner has an expected future lifetime of 18 years. Such disclosure is likely to go on increasing, and trustees will need to be aware of their sponsor's assumptions. Indeed, they ought to be at the table when mortality assumptions are discussed, because it makes no sense for the sponsor to use one set of numbers and the pension fund another.

AND ANOTHER THING

Before we move on to your other advisers, there is one point about actuaries that you must bear in mind. The more you think about it, understand it and know what to do about it, the more effective you can be in your job. Your actuary often sets the discount rate that is used to value your liabilities. I'll repeat that: your actuary sets the discount rate. (Actually, it depends on your Trust Deed – some allow the actuary to set the discount rate, others do not.)

If there is only one thing that causes you to intervene, question and insist upon, it should be discussion of this. By the time you have finished reading this book and have taken on board how to be an effective trustee, that should be eminently clear. For now, please bear in mind that the actuary sets the discount rate.

Whether they set the correct discount rate… is quite another matter. A very few actuaries only ever use the Gilt rate as their chosen discount rate. Others are altogether more ambitious, picking high discount rates that allow companies to understate their liabilities and keep contributions lower than they would otherwise be. Indeed, this practice caused a minor scandal during 2005 when it emerged that actuaries had helped some financially weak companies to do exactly that by using unusually high discount rates (many of these companies also had very high equities exposure). The details are less important than the fact that this will become much harder in future. Why? Because the new regulatory regime is going to put an end to "assumption inflation". Instead, a uniform view of liabilities will be the base for decisions about contribution rates and the speed with which deficits are reduced, and trustees will have a central role to play.

ALL YOU NEED TO KNOW ABOUT BEING A PENSION FUND TRUSTEE

Chapter 5

MAKING UP THE NUMBERS

SPEED-READ SUMMARY

- Investment consultants are to assets what the actuary is to liabilities

- Consultants advise on the appointment and monitoring of your fund managers and on your asset allocation

- Trustees should keep an eye on and seek to avoid transaction costs

- You need to understand what performance numbers actually mean if you are properly to evaluate your investments

- You also need to grapple with some jargon – for instance, you need to know what ALM is and why you should treat it with suspicion

- Important information is often buried in the small print

- Trustees should always ask their consultants to explain things in plain language

When I first became a trustee I was not clear about who did what among our advisers. I could not understand why the actuary answered one set of questions and the consultants another, especially as sometimes the subject matter seemed to overlap. I'm a bit clearer today, so let me try to explain. As ever, I'm favouring simplicity over complexity.

The job of investment consultants is to advise you on how to run the asset side of your pension fund's balance sheet, while the actuary advises on the liabilities side. Given how much we have seen falls on the actuary's plate, you might wonder whether the investment consultants have a lot less to do. But theirs is a vital role. It is your consultants you must turn to when your knowledge and understanding of investment matters reach a limit.

Remember, then:

Liabilities	Assets
Actuaries	Investment Consultants
Statement of Funding Principles	Statement of Investment Principles

But why consultants? Surely you have fund managers who are actually looking after your assets and trying to grow/shelter them, so why can't you deal with them directly? Actually, you can. Under the law, trustees are obliged to hire only an auditor and an actuary – technically, they could choose to do everything else themselves, and that would be fine provided they were fully competent. Investment consultants, like administrators and custodians, are strictly optional. Except that in reality they are rather necessary.

Just to confuse matters, there are some consultants who are also actuaries. These are typically known as "Pensions Consultants" and they have a much broader focus than those who just concentrate on investment advice. In the words of one, a pensions consultant is a "generalist expert who takes on a client management role". But the precise role depends on the business model of the consulting firm. Some bundle all of their services into delivery by a single person/expert. Others separate roles entirely and wheel out separate advisers. This distinction is important, as we will see below. But for the purposes of this chapter I am not going continually to make a distinction – if I write consultant, assume I am covering both possibilities.

But before I explain this in greater detail with reference to your consultants, I must deal with the remaining other advisers who sit around your boardroom table: your scheme administrator and your lawyer.

I could write a lengthy chapter just about these advisers, but it would be worth neither my effort nor your time. Here is what you need to know in a nutshell. There is some donkey-work in running a pension fund and, believe me, you want other people to do it for you. Specialist administrators take care of calculating actual pension payments, running them back through payroll, sending the correct amounts to your fund managers and so on. They have to follow various rules, including the so-called 19-day rule which often comes up as a question when trustees' knowledge is being tested. (I'm going to assume you know what it is!)

If the administrators are competent, then you do not have to waste time worrying about a large area of the fund. So long as you are sure they are competent, let them get on with their job. They are obliged to report back to you regularly, so you should also have a running sense of whether they are doing their job properly. Make sure they are value for money – keep them on their toes by requesting the occasional review of costs. And make sure, if they do mess something up, that you get a satisfactory explanation and an assurance that it will not happen again.

What about your lawyer? I have learned that lawyers hate answering a question with a "yes" or "no", something that severely limits their usefulness. My advice is that you should make sure you ask your lawyer for input if you have a doubt about the legality of something or if you are worried about liability. More often your lawyer will insist on attending so that he can tell you something important about a change in the law or in best practice. Just make sure you ask any questions that occur to you, and also make sure that you have anything important minuted so that there is a record for the future. And if you are in doubt, it never does any harm to ask your lawyer's opinion. A good lawyer will soon tell you whether or not you need his input. And it can help you to get the advice followed up in writing.

With some regularity, you will find that you are asked to take decisions about individual members whose circumstances are unusual in some way. These decisions are important and sometimes quite sensitive. They might involve a colleague's ill health, or an elderly widow who is asking for a pension augmentation. Typically the HR department will be involved.

Curiously it's an area where it is easy to make mistakes because you often do not have the right or complete information. For example, you might get a narrative that a deferred member has cancer and is asking for normal retirement rules to be waived. You need to know what type of cancer and what the medical diagnosis is before you can make a proper decision.

I have two pieces of advice. The first is to ask your advisers, who have seen far more of these cases than you ever will. The second is never to be afraid to ask for more information and time in which to make a decision. In medical cases, of which there are plenty as members get older, it makes a big difference whether someone is dying or is chronically ill. There are easy ways of bypassing the slow timeframe of full trustee meetings to take decisions faster if that is appropriate.

CONSULTING YOUR CONSULTANTS

I noted above that you really need your consultants and advisers. There are several powerful reasons. First, it is not really practical to deal directly with your fund managers. Fund managers speak Martian, and they need interpreting. The average trustee is not equipped to know whether the Martian makes sense or whether it is rubbish designed to cover up failure. Furthermore, fund managers are tenacious. They normally get paid regardless of how well they perform and it is relatively rare for them to get fired soon after they do badly – clients are amazingly slow to react to bad performance. Often it requires a consultant to play bad cop and act as an intermediary who carries out the fund's nasty jobs.

Second, just as actuaries make calculations that trustees could not on their own, so investment consultants do useful tasks that are beyond the technical expertise of almost all trustee boards. As we will see, there are good reasons to be sceptical about a lot of what they do. Indeed, they are as open to criticism in some ways as actuaries have been. But you hire them because you need them, simple as that. Imagine, for a moment that you have dispensed with all of your consultants and are flying entirely on your own. Feels uncomfortable, doesn't it?

Third, beyond the scope of the strict investment consultant role for a moment, there is no sensible trustee board that would want to be its own administrator. The job is painstaking and pernickety, and loaded with potential pitfalls that could trigger complaints and disputes with the Pensions Ombudsman. Unsurprisingly, individual members of pension schemes often care more about the details of their own pensions than they do about far more important issues such as whether trustees got the big decisions right. So lots of trustee boards can find themselves bogged down in lengthy disputes over amazingly trivial matters to do with now-lost pieces of paper that promised xx or yy from an HR director who left 20 years ago. You could spend precious hours dealing with such matters. Far better to outsource the job while making sure that the administrator is properly overseen and audited.

A word of warning. There has been lots of growth and some "consolidation" in the pension-fund consulting business. That means that as firms have become bigger they have also been buying each other in order to get even bigger and, they hope, achieve higher profits because they have greater scale. And consultants have not just bought each other. They have also snapped up firms of actuaries, so that the functions are often for sale from the same company. Today there are three big firms in Britain: Watson Wyatt, Mercers, and Hewitt Bacon & Woodrow. A fourth, smaller firm is Buck, owned by Mellon Bank. In a previous chapter I mentioned Lane Clark & Peacock, another. These firms typically combine a range of services, including broad Human Resources consulting. Also competing in the market are big accounting firms such as KPMG and PricewaterhouseCoopers, which offer actuarial services as well as investment consulting, often to companies as well as to trustee boards.

So you need to ask yourself a question: is your actuary from the same company as your investment consultants? If the answer is "no", then you have avoided one potential conflict of interest that can dog a trustee board. If the (more common) answer is "yes", then you need to give this matter some thought. How you feel about it depends, of course, on the situation of your fund. The worse things look – ie, the bigger the deficit, or the worse relations are with the sponsor – then the more you must think through the issues that might arise from the single view your advisers will be giving you.

Technically there are Chinese walls within firms that combine actuarial and investment consulting services. But these days it's reasonable not to put too much faith in such walls. Recent history suggests they are more honoured in the breach than in the observance. And when the package of services you are selling is quite complex, as it is in this case, it is probably only natural that professionals want to consult with each other to make sure they are essentially in tune. Think about it: it would be extremely embarrassing for both sides if they were to sit in a meeting and offer contradictory advice to the trustees. Just as an actuary who also works for the sponsor spends time sounding out both sides before, often, towing a middle line (or simply following the sponsor's insistence), so the investment consultants and actuary will inevitably work together. This is all the more the case because the investment consulting firms all want to distinguish themselves from their rivals by adopting a particular approach or embracing a particular line.

I'm not saying you should react to this by firing one or other and hiring a replacement from one of the other big firms, although you might decide to do this. I'm saying that you need to be aware of this issue so that you can ask yourself pertinent questions when it comes to the crunch moments during trustee meetings.

Actually, it is possible to mount a plausible defence of why actuaries and consultants should work together, provided they can do so in a way that does not lead to conflict and maintains their independence. As Charles Cowling explains, the actuary needs to know about a fund's strategic asset allocation and ideally needs to be involved in helping to set it. Why? Because it is the actuary who can properly advise on setting the correct quantum of risk for the fund. That really can only be done in tandem with the consultant. The trustees' job is to make sure this is done properly.

A MONITORING SERVICE

But back to investment consultants. The complicated bit of what they do relates to the process around the triennial actuarial review. So let me start with the simpler bit. Investment consultants monitor the performance and reporting of your fund managers. If they do a good job, they tell you how each manager has performed in relation to their stated goals, and how this has affected the overall portfolio. You should bear in mind how this all connects to the Statement of Investment Principles (SIP) that you will have drawn up (or simply signed if you are a new trustee and the job has already been done). For more on the SIP, see the chapters below on investment.

Essentially it is the investment consultants who make sure that you know how closely you are sticking to your SIP and whether there is any need to change something. A drastic change is to sack a fund manager. Less drastic is to divert your new contributions away from one manager to another in order to tilt the balance of the portfolio towards your stated goals. Somewhere in the middle is a decision to switch a chunk of money from one manager to another. Investment consultants advise such switches far more often than they should and this is one of their weak spots. You should avoid switching because a basic and prudent rule of being a trustee is to minimise the transaction costs you pay to investment professionals. You are already paying for the funds to be managed. It is daft to pay even more to switch from one manager to another – unless you really have to, and there will be times when this is the case.

My point is that investment consultants, because they are not paying the bill for switching, tend to suggest it more than they should. Your members ultimately foot the bill, and you should always remember that. (A money-saving tip: if you are moving towards a passive strategy, it is often possible to make the switch away from your active managers for almost zero transaction costs – a few of the big index managers will happily accept a straight transfer of assets, because they just dump them into a huge indexed portfolio that is constantly being rebalanced anyway.)

It is really important that investment consultants present information in a way that you find understandable and useful. This problem is a variation on the actuarial disease of being incomprehensible and out of date by the time information is presented to trustees. You will probably often feel that what the consultant tells you does not really enlighten you very much.

Let me give an example of a common problem. Dig out one of your consultant's investment reports from last year – normally these are quarterly reports and they tend to be reasonably up to date when you first get them because, as I have said, fund managers have almost real-time systems these days and can report down to the minute. If your reports are anything like the ones I used to see, they will show you a bunch of pie charts and bar graphs, with confusing sections on something called asset allocation, probably combined with pages on the performance of individual managers. Can you make much sense of it? I confess I was once thoroughly confused.

GARBAGE IN, GARBAGE OUT

The biggest confusion is as follows. What do you look for when you are monitoring how your assets are faring? Well, you will start by looking at how much you had at the start of the quarter and how much at the end. More is good, less is bad. Let's assume you have more. Cross-check that with the numbers on each manager. The report might say that XX manager outperformed the benchmark by 0.2% in the quarter and is now 0.8% above the benchmark for the year to date. Let's say, by way of example, that in this case all of your managers returned slightly above their benchmarks and, happily, your pool of assets rose from £420 million to £435 million.

Human nature is to think that therefore the managers collectively made £15 million for the fund last quarter – not bad. But did they? Believe it or not, until recently, it was quite difficult to see a picture of your fund that would remind you that, in addition to whatever the fund managers make (or lose), there is new money coming into the fund in the form of new contributions. While the fund managers are managing away, their pools of assets are also being refreshed by new wads of your money. In our hypothetical example, if the sponsoring company was making a £3.5 million contribution each month, then £10.5 million of the increase in assets came from that rather than from investment performance, which actually returned only £4.5m.

Now, a return of £4.5 million might not be bad, even though it is a lot less than £15 million. The point is that as a trustee you have not much clue unless you see the numbers presented in a meaningful way. You need to know how much came in from the company and how much in absolute terms was returned by each manager – the aggregate makes up the total increase in assets over the period. Unless you know this, how on earth can you begin to judge whether each manager is doing a satisfactory job?

I'll tell you: you can't. Rather you need a proper statement of cashflows that shows you exactly what happened to the portfolio over the period in question. If you are not already getting this, then ask for it at once. There is simply no reason other than laziness why investment consultants should present anything other than a clear and helpful view of your portfolio.

A tip: a really useful picture on a quarterly basis is to track your portfolio against your liabilities – how have assets grown relative to your liabilities? This is not a straightforward exercise. For obvious reasons, plenty of assumptions about the liabilities will go into that line on the performance chart. But this way of looking at your fund is much more useful than the traditional view. And more and more investment consultants are offering to present it. If you want to be an effective trustee, then this should be seen as an essential tool with which you can manage your affairs.

A further tip: do you understand the relationship between your contributions and your deficit? It's easy to think that just because there is money coming into your fund that it somehow is automatically reducing your deficit. But it might not be, because deficits grow. Each year there is the effect of the new benefits earned, but there is also, in effect, an interest charge on the existing liabilities. There are also changing assumptions (such as mortality or longevity assumptions) that can increase liabilities. So you need to ask your actuary and advisers to bear this in mind when they report to you. Has the deficit grown or become smaller? Is the fund closer to solvency or further away? If you look only at the money coming in, you might have a rude shock later on.

THE SHAPE OF THINGS TO COME

Further complicating matters is that in addition to the absolute numbers, you need to monitor the overall impact of each manager's performance. This is because you are trying to keep an overall shape to your portfolio. If one manager or group of managers gets too much money or makes super-normal returns, you might find that your portfolio is suddenly bent out of shape.

That needs to be watched because it is one of your duties to stick somewhat close to the parameters set out in your SIP. For example, if you have stipulated in the SIP that you are prepared to accept a moderate degree of risk, which you interpret after taking advice as meaning you can hold 40–50% of your portfolio in the form of equities, then you might have something to explain if the stockmarket crashes and the reduced value of your shares lowers your equity exposure to 25% of your portfolio. You could technically be in breach of trust if you let things become really skewed and you made no change to your SIP and offered no explanation to your members.

Of course, in theory your advisers will never let this happen because they will constantly remind you of your duties. And they tend to like nothing better than suggesting you might "rebalance" your portfolio by a nip here and a tuck there. Yes, we're back to transaction costs again. In the chapters on investment we will return to this because it goes to the heart of one of the thorniest issues facing trustees when they begin to consider their investment strategy – that of benchmarks. What is important to absorb here is that you don't have to follow your consultant's advice all of the time. In fact, you can often do a better job for members by quizzing your advisers and then making up your own mind.

THE BIG PICTURE

I said above that the complicated part of the investment consultant's job is to work in parallel with the triennial actuarial review and produce for the assets side of the balance sheet an equivalent to the actuary's guidance on liabilities. Strictly speaking, that is truer of the recent past than it is of today. As we noted in the previous chapter, actuaries have had to become more flexible and run almost rolling valuations of funds, especially those in deficit. But the old practice remains relevant because although the timing might be changing the process is essentially the same.

Now, to make the most of this chapter, I suggest you go to your files and dig out a copy of your most recent big report from your investment consultants. If this turns out to be about a fund manager or a performance review, then put it back. I suggest you look to see whether your scheme has done something called an "Investment strategy and asset/liability modelling" report, or words to that effect – look above all for the words "Asset" and "Liability". This is normally a thick document of up to 50 or 60 pages and it should be dated around the same time as your last formal actuarial review. Indeed, it should say right at the beginning (often an Executive Summary) something along the lines of "this report is produced in light of the actuarial valuation carried out in xx month xx year".

A note: not every trustee board, particularly smaller ones, will commission ALM studies – often it is felt they are not justified given the costs. So if you are in that position, you might skip the next few pages. Actually I'd recommend that you read on regardless, because I hope the analysis below will be useful to all trustees.

Before you read on, glance through the investment and asset-liability modelling (ALM) report. I know I keep asking these questions, but how much of it do you understand? I have asked around and can confidently say that only a minority of trustees even read such reports, let alone understand them. You only have to see words such as "stochastic" and "scenario" for your eyes to glaze over. I talked with one trustee who personally sat in a meeting where it became obvious that she was the only trustee to have done anything more than skim a major investment ALM report.

In fact, it was the process of hearing about how she read that report in detail that really made me think properly about becoming an effective trustee. Although they were unpopular and a little uncomfortable in the asking, the questions she tabled in the subsequent meeting of the trustee board laid the ground for a major overhaul of the fund in question and also set in motion much faster funding of a deficit by the sponsoring company. So you see, it can be done.

I have seen several ALM reports from a variety of funds and they make depressingly similar reading. It can also be an odd experience reading them, because they contain so many assumptions and statements that have been debunked by the new actuaries, yet remain the common parlance of consultants. I should also point out that a lot of things are changing – what a consultant wrote last year can often look completely out of date, given the impact of the Pensions Regulator on the industry. However, a lot of the underlying assumptions remain, so it is still vital that you understand where your consultants are coming from.

Of course, not all consultants are the same. I know of several who think ALM reports are a complete waste of time, but who then raise a caveat: there are bits of a typical ALM report that have the potential to be useful, but they are often done wrongly or are ignored because no one can see them through the dross. I will elaborate on this below.

ALL IN FOR ALM

The following analysis is based on a report from 2004 that was shown to me by a frustrated trustee of a largish fund. I have changed all of the numbers and mixed up a lot of the language in order to preserve the trustees' anonymity, so that any one of the big consultants could read the text below and not be sure whether it came from them. What follows is a detailed description of the report that I have peppered with remarks to show where an effective trustee might reasonably dispute what looks on the surface like a sensible analysis. The goal here is to prove that anyone who makes the effort can understand even the most forbidding report – it just takes time and a little bit of knowledge.

First, some basics. Remember that most funds, and this one is no exception, are stuffed full of equities, are closed to new members and have deficits. And remember that your duty as a trustee is to your members, not to the sponsoring company.

A natural starting point for your investment consultant is to review your situation in a short "Executive Summary", normally a page or two of brief statements. This is simple enough. On xx date, based on the actuary's recent valuation, your fund is xx% funded. There are different ways of judging a funding level and the recommended way has been changing in recent years. Most trustees will have wrestled with FRS17, the account standard which recently replaced SSAP24. All should be aware of the MFR (Minimum Funding Requirement), which is another measure, set down by the Pensions Act 1995. Many will also have come across the idea of measuring funding on a so-called solvency basis (this is my preferred measure and I will explain this more in the chapters below). In this case, the consultant wrote that:

"On January 1 2004 the fund was 69.4% funded on the Actuary's ongoing valuation basis and approximately 91% funded on an MFR basis."

Here is my first criticism of many. Note that 69.4% is presented as a definite number, while a rounded number is described as approximate. Is this because the actuary is so clever that his number is unquestionable? Or is this merely a false precision by the consultant? The latter, I think. After all, remember what we saw in the previous chapter about the heroic assumptions actuaries make when they undertake a valuation. In addition, the statement above assumes that the trustees will understand the differences between the funding approaches. Do you? It is actually quite a complicated issue that is subject to ongoing change, and this statement makes no mention of FRS17, another funding measure and the one that has been given greater weight in the regime set up by the Pensions Act and the new Regulator. Wouldn't it be better if the consultant spelled this out more clearly? Would the above prose tell you which of the two the consultant thinks is the more meaningful measure? I thought not.

The next statement is remarkable:

"We believe there is scope to continue to regard return maximisation subject to controlling to some extent the risks relative to the fund's liabilities as one of the trustees' key objectives."

Put aside the fact that this is badly written and uses jargon ("return maximisation") to mystify. Just think about what this is saying in light of what we know to be trustees' duties and responsibilities. Here is a paid consultant saying that as a main objective the trustees should continue to try to pursue the highest returns they can, ie, take risks by holding lots of equities. But the advice is confused by what follows. Trustees must do this "subject to controlling to some extent" those risks. What does that mean? Perhaps it means that the trustees should not take excessive risks, given that they have liabilities to consider. But to "some" extent? What extent? A little or a lot? When you begin to unpack the language, you start to wonder whether the sentence means anything at all.

Finally, the consultant proffers the following:

"Our main recommendation is that the current asset allocation (of 80% equities and 20% bonds) remains appropriate, although we recognise that it is at the more aggressive end of the range of reasonable asset allocation policies."

What should a trustee make of that? Your consultant is telling you to stick with what you have, but is also pointing out that you are right on the edge of "reasonable" behaviour. Surely as a trustee you want to be as close to reasonable as possible? Otherwise don't you risk a lawsuit from your members? The last thing you can possibly endorse is anything that smacks of recklessness. But apparently an almost reckless asset allocation "remains appropriate". Why? Was it ever appropriate, and why should it be so? This is simply taken for granted by the consultant. But these are the kinds of questions you absolutely must ask, not just to yourself or your fellow trustees, but to your investment consultants as well.

I hope it is already clear that an effective trustee can go a long way just by reading carefully the most innocuous of documents. Yet most trustees would have read the executive summary, part of which is quoted above, and not blinked an eyelid. Further, they would not have read the remaining 55 pages of the report, so would have had no basis for asking even more probing questions. But let's assume you have read only the passages I quote above. They ought to be enough to set alarm bells ringing about the quality of the advice you receive. If you do read on, you need ear protectors.

THE DEVIL IN THE DETAILS

The ALM report goes on to say, by way of introduction, that it:

"enables us to compare and contrast different investment scenarios in light of the trustees' and Employer's attitude to risk so a clear understanding is gained of the potential impact of future outcomes…"

"The recommended benchmarks necessarily take into account our understanding of the trustees' (and the Employer's) attitudes to risk and return. In particular, we note the Employer's view that the current asset allocation is appropriate given the preliminary valuation results and that they are not inclined to move to an unduly conservative position."

Does anything strike you so far? What struck me most is that the investment consultant whose bill you are paying seems more concerned to kowtow to the employer than to tell you honestly and straightforwardly what you should be doing. Just read the language again, because the more you read it the more troubling it becomes. It would be one thing for the company to let you know via a communication that it preferred the trustees to keep on taking risks with a high equity exposure. It is quite another for your own paid adviser to do exactly the same job. Check your own most recent ALM study and see whether it contains anything similar. The consultant should be on your side, not trimming between you and the employer.

Some consultants might baulk at this. Surely, they might argue, it is indeed part of their job to help the trustees to adopt a reasonable position, and that must include an awareness of where the employer stands. True. But that assumes that trustees are incapable of communicating themselves with the employer. Given the presence of so many finance directors and other company representatives on most trustee boards, most such communication is anyway done fairly directly. The language above strongly suggests, rather than hints, that this consultant has crossed a line.

The ALM report then moves on to talk about investment strategy. As we will discuss this in subsequent chapters, I will pass over this section fairly quickly. However, this is a good point to set the reader a challenge. Here are some brief extracts. The challenge is to anticipate my analysis of them. Read the paragraphs below and make a note every time something strikes you:

"The starting point in assessing an appropriate asset allocation strategy is to consider the least risk option. A correctly specified portfolio of fixed-interest and index-linked bonds can significantly reduce investment risk within a pension scheme's investment arrangements and is, in our view, the least risk portfolio available to trustees.

… The major drawback to investing wholly in such a portfolio is that bonds are expected to give lower returns than other asset classes, particularly equities. Whilst investment in bonds is therefore the least risk option, such an approach is likely to make the long-term cost of the scheme more expensive to the Employer, potentially prohibitively so. To manage this cost, trustees have found it appropriate to consider some exposure to equities. This is on the key assumption, however, that the sponsor would support the scheme should the expected enhanced performance fail to materialise.

… The correct equity exposure for a scheme should reflect the degree of risks the trustees are comfortable with within their investment arrangements taking all factors into account (including the interests of the sponsoring employer).

Finally, we note that the benefit of this expected excess return, if it materialises, can then manifest itself in two key ways, namely in the form of reduced contribution requirements and/or in the form of benefit payments over and above that guaranteed."

MARKS OUT OF TEN?

OK let's stop there. There is a danger that too much of this stuff has the same effect as the real thing – you just want to stop reading it. Remember that this is just a series of extracts. The actual text ran to several pages. But I hope by now, you are jumping on certain words and phrases and spotting immediately that they are deeply suspect. Either they are flawed intellectually or they reveal how conflicted the consultant is in its advice. How many problematic points did you spot? And how many points were valid? Give yourself marks according to each item in italics below that you correctly identified.

"The starting point in assessing an appropriate asset allocation strategy is to consider the least risk option. A correctly specified portfolio of fixed-interest and index-linked bonds can significantly reduce investment risk within a pension scheme's investment arrangements and is, in our view, the least risk portfolio available to trustees. *Amazing – the consultant has actually written something correct. Actually, the first sentence is even more correct today than it was when it was written, because the advice from the Pensions Regulator is precisely along these lines. (1 mark)*

… The major drawback to investing wholly in such a portfolio is that bonds are expected to give lower returns than other asset classes, particularly equities. *Have you heard that somewhere before? Of course you have. We are slap-bang in "new actuary" territory here. Note also that the consultant positions the idea of a portfolio that is "wholly" invested in bonds. This sets the trap in the next sentence. (2 marks)* Whilst investment in bonds is therefore the least risk option, such an approach is likely to make the long-term cost of the scheme more expensive to the Employer, potentially prohibitively so. *Where to start? See how the unrealistic assumption of an entire portfolio of bonds now justifies the assertion that this would be too expensive? In practice, only the Boots pension fund ever went entirely into bonds, although arguably most others should have done so. Note the implicit warning to the trustees that the consultant has a pretty good idea that the employer will not tolerate too many bonds. (2 marks)* To manage this cost, trustees have found it appropriate to consider some exposure to equities. *Since when did serious exposure to equities of on average above 60% of assets become "some" exposure? This so seriously distorts reality that you wonder where the consultant is going. Note also that trustees did not invest in equities in order to manage "this cost", ie, the cost of holding too many bonds – they held equities because they did not know any better and because the entire advisory industry encouraged them to do so. (1 mark)* This is on the key assumption, however, that the sponsor would support the scheme should the expected enhanced performance fail to materialise. *Whoa, did you get that? The consultant is saying that if you hold lots of equities because they are expected to produce juicy returns, then you had better have a parachute in the form of support through thick and thin from the employer just in case they don't. This could have been presented as really good advice, as it plays directly to the question of the employer's covenant. Sadly, however, it was simply glossed over. Although I did not give the extract here, the report moved on immediately to explain to the trustees just how much more a bond-based approach would cost. (1 mark)*

… The correct equity exposure for a scheme should reflect the degree of risks the trustees are comfortable with within their investment arrangements taking all factors into account (including the interests of the sponsoring employer). *What on earth is that bracket doing there? Whose side is the consultant on? (1 mark)*

Finally, we note that the benefit of this expected excess return, if it materialises, can then manifest itself in two key ways, namely in the form of reduced contribution requirements and/or in the form of benefit payments over and above that guaranteed." *What planet is the consultant on? Once again, the report conflates the interests of the trustees with those of the company. The trustees are largely indifferent to the future level of contributions, provided they have done an effective job in maximising the funding level today. As for the idea of augmented benefits, it reads like a sick joke. Any fund with a deficit is facing reduced benefits unless the hole can be plugged. And there is more and more good advice available to trustees to suggest that holding lots of equities is a highly risky way of trying to plug a hole – so risky that it is not in members' interests. Do your members really want you to gamble with their money? How would they feel if they knew what was really going on? (2 marks)*

How did you get on? Anything over five marks out of ten is probably progress! If you scored less than that, and you can face it, you need to tune up your critical faculties.

ASSUMPTIONS, ASSUMPTIONS

In a book of this nature it is impossible to be comprehensive. In fact, it's important that the content is not comprehensive, because then the book would have little chance of achieving its aim. You will see below in the chapters on investment that I have been economical with a subject that has filled entire libraries. And it is tempting at this point to move on, having suggested a few ways that you might challenge your consultants by understanding better what they do.

In this case, however, I think it would be wrong to move on. There are other extremely confusing aspects of the consultant's advice. If you don't understand them, then your effectiveness will be quite limited, because you will not see the entire picture. That matters because it will be only too easy for a consultant to respond to a query by lobbing in a few complications that leave you befuddled, even if you were on the right track.

A short example? Say you raise a question about the asset-allocation framework the consultant has been setting out above. You might have a perfectly valid point that the advice looks biased towards equities. What do you do if your consultant answers something like: "Thank you for that interesting question. Actually, according to our stochastic analysis there is a 65% probability that equities will make sufficient excess return over the next decade to close the deficit and only a 5% probability that they will underperform, and I can assure you that the sponsor has indicated during the actuarial valuation that it is happy to see the trustees stick with the current asset-allocation policy which is no way biased etc etc."?

Effectively, you're floored. Unless you have the technical tools to take on the consultant there is not much you can say to this. That is why I am going to carry on with this chapter. We need to unpick the consultant's processes a bit further. It's the only way to make sure that when you do begin to take decisions you are as well informed as possible.

INSIDE THE BLACK BOX

A common difficulty with investment consultants is that it is often difficult, nay impossible, to know what they are really advising. They often hedge their bets, appearing to advise one thing, but then hiding contradictory advice elsewhere in their report. That way they can escape charges of giving bad advice! Let me give another real example. In the case of one small pension fund, the consultant made what appeared to be an unequivocal recommendation:

"We believe that... a minimum exposure to equity type assets of around 40% would be required... "

Buried in the report, however, commenting on the fund's 60% equity allocation, the consultant noted:

"It is evident... that there is a significant mismatch between the Fund's assets and its underlying ongoing liabilities... "

Now, you might think you can take this with a pinch of salt. Any good adviser should show you the full range of possible courses of action, and explain the merits of each measured against the others. A degree of hedging of bets is inevitable. True, but there are limits. In the end you need reasonable information so that you can make considered decisions. Even if you have to fight for it, you should try to get a clear answer from your consultant, rather than allow such obfuscation. This is particularly true when it comes to some of the more technical tricks consultants use. Let's turn in some detail to the ALM process itself. Most consultants divide this into two phases. They run a series of scenarios of what might happen in the future, first using a *deterministic* method, then using a *stochastic* method.

Those two words are enough to stop most trustees in their tracks. Do not worry, they are easy to understand once you learn a few basics.

First, you do not need to worry overly about the deterministic approach. It is mostly rubbish, because it consists of the consultants plucking four or five economic scenarios out of the air and seeing what these might mean for your fund. I think the process is worthless and I'm not alone. If you read carefully what the consultants say about their scenarios, often you will find the analysis is flawed or just plain silly (and often you will find that a detailed description of the scenarios is buried deep in an appendix).

For example, it has been quite common for consultants to include a scenario called "Boom". In this lovely future, everything goes swimmingly and equities do wonderfully well. Is that really a useful way of thinking about the future? It certainly will not tell you very much if you follow the consultant's next step, which is to see what happens to various asset mixes under each scenario. It should come as no surprise that a portfolio containing 100% equities will do beautifully under Boom, whereas a 100% bond portfolio would look less attractive (this, of course, assumes that maximising returns is your goal, whereas you might quite reasonably choose to minimise risk).

DETERMINEDLY DETERMINISTIC

My strong advice is not to pay much heed to a deterministic analysis, assuming one is offered to you. Weak scenarios are one justification. Another is that the deterministic approach lacks an essential ingredient: each scenario is presented as equally likely. We know in real life that that cannot be the case. We also know that it is impossible to forecast the future accurately. State-of-the-art thinking in fund management is that when we make a forecast, the only thing we can be certain of is that our forecast will be wrong, so that the relevant question is "By how much?" But investment advisers ignore such niceties.

Instead, they undertake a stochastic analysis. Meaning what, exactly? Ironically the word derives from Greek for aiming at a mark or guessing! A more modern definition is "pertaining to conjecture". In the investment world, however, stochastic analysis refers to a statistical technique that measures the distribution of a series of random outcomes in order to see whether there is some overall predictability. That is not very clear, is it? Let's look at an example.

Take the price of a single share in X Corporation. Each trading day it moves randomly up or down by a certain amount. If we keep accurate records, we can chart how it moves over time. A simple measure is to set the axis at zero (ie, the price is unchanged) and then to plot daily moves into positive or negative territory. Do this for long enough and the random price changes begin to settle down into what looks like a pattern of sorts – we can see that the share most often moves up or down by a single penny, but occasionally makes more dramatic moves. We can even draw this and analyse the likelihood that on a given day the value of the share will alter by a particular amount. Note that we do not know for sure what will happen on that day, only what is most likely to happen. But we can say, with some certainty, for example, that a one-penny move happens 60% of the time, whereas a twenty-penny move happens on average only 1% of the time. If we do this, we are conducting a stochastic analysis.

UPS AND DOWNS

The same model is applied to pension funds, but with some peculiar twists as we will see.

So let's go back to our consultants and see what they do next:

"[We use] a simulation of 1,000 possible economic scenarios... By considering the spread of results over all simulations, it is possible to estimate the possibility of various events occurring... The best and worst 5% of the results are omitted from the output, although it is important to be aware that extreme situations can occur and hence the outer limits of the results shown do not represent the best and worst possible outcomes."

Now, this looks as if it makes some sense. What the consultant is saying is that the analysis will start from the position today – the level of the scheme's funding and how much contribution the employer is paying – and project it forward across a wide range of possible future scenarios. As trustees, you will be presented with the distribution of outcomes, but with the extremes at each end cut off.

That sounds reasonable enough until you consider one thing: the extremes are what matter, in pension funds as in life. To see why, go back to the share example above. You would probably assume that on a given day the shares are more likely to move by a penny than by more than twenty pennies. But if you were betting your house on a single day's move, you would certainly focus on the small possibility that there might be a fall of more than twenty pennies and consider your wager twice. And if you were assessing how big your deficit might be in future, you should certainly consider the best and worst outcomes. It is simply bizarre to make an arbitrary cutting off of the edges of the distribution (known in the industry as the "tails"). Even more bizarre is the consultant's assertion that "extreme situations can occur" – surely these are the ones that matter? An insurance analogy helps. Would you buy a home insurance policy that would pay for repairs after a small fire that was confined to your kitchen, but would not pay if your entire house burned down? Exactly.

At this stage of the investment consultant's ALM report you will probably be presented with lots of colourful charts showing you how the various projections of your current position (including your current asset allocation) look over the next few years. These can be quite confusing, but actually they are not as nasty as they look. The top and bottom points we know will represent the 95% and 5% cut-offs (because 5% at each end has been excluded). The central point is known as the "median" and is a common reference point. Other typical slices occur at 25% (the lower quartile) and 75% (the upper quartile). Remember, what you are seeing are projections of how your portfolio today might look tomorrow.

You might then see some text as follows:

"It can be seen from the charts that the median funding level after five years is around 85%. This is expected to rise thanks to higher contributions by the employer and to a slightly higher investment return from the scheme's assets than assumed in the actuarial valuation. There is also a potential upside with a 25% chance that the funding level will be in excess of 99% and a 5% chance of it being above 120%. However, on the downside, there is a 25% chance of a funding level below 74% and a 5% chance of this falling below 60%."

RUBBER STAMP TIME

What on earth does all that mean? Reading it you can see why trustees tend to give up and reach for the rubber stamp. I urge you not to react this way. It is remarkably easy to be effective against such presentation. Here's how. First of all, note that we are back in the land of fantasy and imagination – having told us that the top and bottom 5% of results are excluded, the consultant promptly throws them back in, and enticingly so. Someone who wanted to be positive and to keep the portfolio unchanged might be quite upbeat about that 5% chance of overfunding. But of course, the important point is that the median funding level is still only 85%, which represents significant underfunding. Remember that this is a portfolio stuffed full of equities – 80% of the assets are held in shares.

Second, it is possible to extract a lot more information from this analysis if you know how. It lies in the upside and downside idea. Go back to the text above. It is striking, though not at all obvious, that there are some equal and opposite odds mentioned. For instance, there is the same 25% chance that the scheme will have funding "in excess of 99%" and "below 74%". Equally, there is a 5% likelihood of overfunding to the point where the company might renew a contribution holiday, and underfunding serious enough that it might put the overall survival of the fund in jeopardy.

This takes on extra meaning when the consultant's second variable is put alongside it: what happens to the expected level of company contributions under the different scenarios? (Bear in mind that each outcome translates into a different future funding requirement, and the operating assumption is that the better the funding level the lower the amount needed as future contributions.) The ALM report goes on as follows:

"The median [contribution amount] required after five years is approximately £35.8 million. This is a marginal increase from the calculated ongoing rate of £33.5 million. The favourable outcomes are contribution amounts of £15 million with a 25% chance and £12.5 million with a 5% chance. There is a 25% possibility of a contribution amount in excess of £50 million, and a 5% chance that this will be above £65 million."

The point buried in all these numbers is that there are tangible financial effects of different outcomes in future that have a direct bearing on your fund. The high equity weighting (80%) produces some outcomes that look good for the sponsoring company because they have the potential to bring the contribution rate down to a manageable £15 million, less than half the current rate. But there is an equal chance (risk) that the contribution rate will have to go up substantially, so much so that there would be real questions over the ongoing strength of the employer's covenant at that level. Put another way, that would look terrible for your members. Remember them? It's easy to forget them when you are stuck in the mire of a typical ALM report.

It is quite useful for a trustee to be able to weigh up these upside and downside possibilities, while always remembering that the actual outcome will be different. Are you comfortable with the idea that there is a 5% chance that things will be very badly wrong? Is there a level of disaster at which you feel reasonably sure the company will be reluctant to bail the fund out? What might happen to that number if you altered your asset allocation to make your fund less risky? It is also worth re-asking the questions I raised in Chapter Four. How much can your sponsoring company afford to pay, and how much is it willing to pay? The strength of that covenant is vital to your effectiveness.

REAL NUMBERS WANTED

That is the next layer of complication in a typical ALM report. The next stage is to start presenting a range of portfolios with different asset allocations. It is not uncommon for these to start with a 100% equity portfolio and end with a 100% bond portfolio, with big (20% or 25%) increments in between. If your consultant does this, I suggest you ask why. It makes no sense at all to include completely unrealistic portfolios in the analysis – they serve only to confuse or to confirm what we know intuitively to be true, eg, if you have 100% equities, you have a small chance of blowing the roof off, but an equal chance of losing your shirt.

A much better (though sadly rare) approach is for the consultant to model portfolios that are realistic having asked the trustees for some guidance. This is a radical thought. Why are consultants so reluctant to ask questions before they do their detailed number crunching? It would make far more sense. Consider a trustee board wondering what to do about its 65% equity exposure. If the consultant asked, it might turn out that the trustees want to compare alternatives with equity holdings of, say, 55%, 50%, 45% and 40%, with an outlier at 20%. Alternatively, the trustees might say they want a radical shift away from equities to a range of 15–30%, so it would be appropriate to model only within this. But the consultant can know this only if he asks.

Somewhere in your ALM report are vital figures, if only you can find them. One is the probability assigned to a favourable outcome based on your current portfolio mix. In this case, it turns out that there is a one in three chance that the contribution rate will fall to £15 million or less. Another is the probability assigned to a nasty outcome. Lo and behold, it turns out there is a one in three chance that the contribution rate will rise to more than £50 million. But to grasp this essential nugget, you have to search carefully. And to appreciate it, you have first to have waded through an awful lot of dross.

ALMOST THERE

I want to end this marathon chapter with one final example of fine consultant thinking. Here goes, from the appendices of an actual ALM report:

"Most commentators continue to expect equities to outperform bonds in the future to compensate for the additional risk associated with equity investment. Following the excesses of the 1990s however the consensus is that the additional return from equities is likely to be lower than has been the case historically... Before setting out our expectations we note that actual future equity returns are of course very dependent on the initial level of equity markets one starts from, which makes forecasting in the current volatile markets doubly difficult."

By now every reader should be able to see this for the specious nonsense that it is. Andrew Smithers, an investment commentator with a sharp wit and lively mind, made the following apposite observation: "The unusual nature of the current approach to pension funding is not that it assumes that risks will be rewarded, but that it records the profit on those risks with foresight rather than hindsight."

Quite. An effective trustee will know this to be the case and ask every awkward question possible to fight for a clearer picture.

AND FINALLY...

It should be clear by now that your relationship with your consultant is pretty important – it touches on so many areas of your responsibilities. Yet I have looked around for helpful advice to trustees and come up with precious little. The NAPF publishes a worthy booklet of 26 pages called "A guide to good practice", but it's one of those volumes that is remarkably uninformative because it simply does not describe the relationships in practice. Worse, it distracts attention from the main issues by going into great detail about how trustees can use a "balanced score card" approach to evaluate their consultants.

One thing it does show is that the range of advice now given by consultants is much wider than it was 30 years ago when pension funds tended to choose from an extremely narrow selection of investment vehicles. It also has an intriguing section on risk, which argues that trustees can take risk over time, but should do so only if they have a clear understanding (here called "a strong level of comfort") with the sponsoring employer that a consequence might be "a variable contribution level". My practical advice on that is to note that this is a very big "if".

ALL YOU NEED TO KNOW ABOUT BEING A PENSION FUND TRUSTEE

Chapter 6

NOW IT GETS INTERESTING

SPEED-READ SUMMARY

- Trustees can make a real difference if they know what their powers are and how to use them

- Everyone should study the WH Smith case as a model for how trustees can influence events to the benefit of scheme members

- As Martin Taylor says, pension deficits are loans "acquired without consent from a uniquely vulnerable lender"

- The new regulatory regime under David Norgrove is hugely helpful to trustees who want to be effective

- The guidance on "Clearance" is a vital document for trustees

- Trustees need to evaluate the financial health of the sponsoring company

- Healthy companies can and do go bust very quickly

- Trustees have to be confident in working together with the sponsor – they need to establish their position and be prepared to stick to it

- Consider asking for security in case things go wrong

Well, I had to do something to keep you reading. I have written so much about your two main advisory relationships because your effectiveness as a trustee depends very much on your understanding of what they do. This chapter looks at how trustees have had to become more assertive and why the regulatory environment is shifting in their favour.

The essence of this chapter stands for this book as a whole: you really can make a difference. Indeed, it is increasingly expected that you will make a difference. There are more and more precedents for trustees becoming more decisive and acting more effectively to safeguard and secure their members' interests. Some are well known, but still worth describing and analysing because trustees can only gain wisdom from studying them. Others are less public, but no less important for that.

If you ask the informed man in the street about the corporate pensions crisis, chances are he will have heard of Boots' switch into bonds and the case involving the trustees of WH Smith, the troubled high-street retailing group. Boots is dealt with at length in the next chapter – in my view, it is the flagship case for trustees becoming effective on the investment side of their responsibilities, and it also sheds interesting light on the conflicts of interest issue.

In the WH Smith case, a trustee board became effective on what we might call "broad governance". The fund had the typical characteristics that have created so many headaches for trustees, ie, a big deficit, riddled with potential conflicts of interest, etc. More importantly, it found itself at the centre of a battle for control of the sponsoring company. It is therefore emblematic of the way in which pension funds have moved from being an off-balance-sheet bore to an essential element of how companies perceive and manage their balance sheets.

We are fortunate to have had an extremely articulate participant in the form of Martin Taylor, former boss of Barclays. He was chairman of WH Smith's trustee board only by dint of his being chairman of the company as a whole. Mr Taylor does not need me to paraphrase for him – he is an elegant writer and speaker. In May 2005 he gave a keynote address to the National Association of Pension Funds (NAPF) annual conference in which he outlined his experience when WH Smith was approached by a private-equity investor with an eye to a takeover. He also usefully set out what he saw as the main lessons for trustees and the industry as a whole. With his permission, I have included in italics an extracted version below:

My experience at WH Smith last summer was an object lesson in what a nuisance it can be to be a pension fund trustee. What I intend to do is relate the story of the WH Smith-Permira encounter last year from the trustee viewpoint, and discuss some of the conclusions I have drawn from it.

In 1999 I became chairman of WH Smith, which automatically also made me chairman of trustees of the WH Smith Fund. These roles had been combined for a quarter of a century, which was, under modern governance standards, an uncomfortable compromise, and when a large deficit emerged during 2001/2002, it became impossible to sustain. I had, however, decided to step down from chairing the board, and by remaining as pension fund chairman I could help the company effect the necessary governance switch. The deficit, by the way, was in the order of £215m – see below.

As chairman of both, I used to think, "well, this is uncomfortable, and maybe a touch improper, but how lucky everyone is to have someone like me, who can balance conflicting views and find a compromise at the perfect point of rest". I know now that that position was ridiculous. To have to consider the interests of the beneficiaries exclusively has been good for me, and therefore good for them.

My first conclusion is this: those of you who are directors of the sponsoring company as well as trustees should resign at once from one position or the other. At once. This is splendid advice, but to date has been little heeded and would probably cause difficulties for many funds, which would struggle to cope with a mass exodus of trustees. A further question occurs to me, though. Why stop at directors? What about the head of HR, who is below director level, but is nevertheless a senior company officer...

At the time of which I am speaking – the spring of 2004 – the market cap of the company was around £700–800 million. That was roughly the same size as the liability of the scheme on an FRS17 basis. The gross deficit on this measure was around £200 million – on a more stringent measure a good deal higher. So the fund was not only in deficit, but also very large compared with the company. Large by any standard, but some big companies have even bigger deficits. Note that Mr Taylor appears to be referring either directly to the FRS17 company accounting basis, or, more obliquely, to the solvency measure when he mentions a "more stringent" measure. More and more leading thinkers in the pensions industry are thinking that the solvency measure is the correct way to view a fund in deficit. The move is one away from the "ongoing actuarial" view of deficits.

The trustees had powers to set contributions – not entirely unilaterally, but very strong powers nevertheless – and to wind the scheme up if the company ever misbehaved. Powers of this nature are increasingly within the grasp of all trustee groups, following recent legislation. The WH Smith trustees' ability to set contribution rates is a relatively unusual power. Some Trust Deeds also allow the sponsoring company to fire a trustee board and replace it with a "Special trustee" who can remake policy. And many companies in practice control the contribution rate by making it clear to trustees (often via the actuary or consultant) that they are prepared to pay only so much. However, Mr Taylor's point is surely correct – trustees do have more, and more effective, power and they should not be afraid to use it. Moreover, even if the Trust Deed does not give trustees the explicit power to set contributions, the new regulatory regime gives them considerably expanded powers – if they do not like a proposed contribution rate on the grounds that it is inadequate, trustees can refer to the Regulator, which can impose a contribution level to which the company must adhere.

My second conclusion is this: possession of power entails the responsibility to use it; and to use it wisely. Failure to act when you are able to can be construed as negligent. Trustees should act, not wring their hands. Which begs the question why many do not. The answer is a combination of fear (that they will annoy their employer, which typically has representatives sitting right there at the table with them), ignorance (including among members who should know more about their power to pressure trustees into action) and sloth (it is remarkably easy to let a year pass in which nothing effective is done). The longer I have been a trustee and the more trustees I have talked to, the more it appears that fear is the most important of these factors. Sponsoring companies are not afraid to push their own preferences and agendas on to trustees, but for too long it has been implied or actually stated that trustees who push back are somehow being confrontational and are thereby jeopardising members' interests. Of course, this view would have more weight if there were clear evidence that the sponsor was acting responsibly and efficiently in its management of the pension fund.

Permira approached WH Smith in March 2004 and asked it to perform due diligence as a preliminary to – potentially – bidding for the company. The board agreed, and the pension fund became part of this process. I should mention at this point that I was conflicted in every direction: past chairman of the company, responsible for appointing its new chief executive officer, whom Permira incidentally sought to replace, shareholder, chairman of trustees and adviser to the firm that was itself advising Permira. These egregious conflicts were generally considered to net out to zero, so I carried on – though I naturally had no contact with the relevant Goldman Sachs people, and no contact either with the company management except as strictly required to discuss their defence plans. We trustees kept the company and Permira at exactly the same distance: the future ownership of the company was not our business. The safety of the pension fund was our only business. It is rare, but refreshing, to see a senior business figure be so frank about conflicts of interest. Note, however, that it was something of a leap of faith to reach the netting out to zero position! Trustee boards might adopt as a motto the phrase "The safety of the pension fund is our only business".

Third conclusion: trustees are not an extension of the corporate management and must act independently in a contested situation.

I was enormously helped by having not only an honourable, thoughtful and hardworking bunch of member trustees, but two independents of great experience and ability. Without Louise Botting and Jeremy Stone I doubt we could have got through. My fourth conclusion, therefore, is that any trustee chairman who doesn't avail him or herself of good independent trustees is potty. Remember Chapter One? Trustees are there to serve the members of the fund, not the sponsoring employer. I note that Mr Taylor singles out both the member trustees and independents, but makes no mention of employer-appointed trustees. But his use of the term "extension of corporate management" makes his position pretty clear.

Permira intended, of course, to pile debt into the capital structure, and we would have been sitting right at the bottom. The bankruptcy risk was not huge, but nor was it negligible. The company had few assets to "cut up" on liquidation, and – had it failed – we would have been left with a very substantial real deficit. Although we had no concerns about Permira's willingness to service the pension fund as part of a going concern, we clearly could not accept this. We therefore demanded some mixture of a) up-front coverage of the pension deficit by a cash injection; b) ranking pari passu with secured creditors for any remaining deficit; c) guarantee backed by other assets of Permira and its co-investors. This was an extremely brave and sensible course and offers a general lesson to trustees. You do not have to think in terms of blocking any move by a predator or your sponsor. But you do have to consider the consequences, and then fight to make sure the fund's interests are preserved, in the form of either sufficient hard cash to reduce the deficit to a manageable and acceptable level or a strengthened covenant with the employer/acquirer.

At the same time, the company had shared with us its defence plans, which involved selling a major division and returning cash to shareholders. From our point of view this would clearly have shrunk the company and weakened its covenant, so we stipulated a substantial one-off payment under these circumstances (which we have now received) of £120 million. Note the importance of seeing the picture in the round – in seeking to defend itself, the company might have damaged the fund's interests just as much as a hostile acquirer.

Our intention was to treat both management and bidder even-handedly; our only grounds for discrimination between them were a function of their different capital structures. A model approach.

Fifth conclusion: people more learned than I am are fond of discussing the exact credit and security standing of the pension creditor. For me, a deficit in the pension scheme is an irregular situation that should not persist. All trustees have the responsibility of working out with the sponsor how this debt is to be repaid, and how quickly. There is no point bankrupting the sponsor, but you need to behave like an intelligent banker. Pension deficits are unpaid wages, looked at one way, or a loan acquired without consent from a uniquely vulnerable lender. This neatly and succinctly sums up the position adopted by the Pensions Regulator – see below for a more detailed discussion.

Eventually Permira pulled out, not because it could not reach agreement with the trustees, but because it realised the cost of such an agreement would force it to lower its bid to a level at which it did not expect to succeed. We can argue about whether this means that the equity market was not correctly valuing the pension fund deficit. WH Smith had certainly provided ample information to the market on this subject. But there still seem to be people out there who think these liabilities are in some way unreal or at least overstated. In my opinion this is unlikely to change drastically until there have been further test cases and trustees have shown just how effective they can be in complex situations.

My sixth conclusion, therefore, is this: trustees and finance directors must have no illusions about the size of the deficit. The actuarial convention according to which the composition of the assets determines the size of the liabilities is one of the weirdest emanations of the human mind. It's a metaphor – like saying that the advent of jet planes made the Atlantic narrower – and metaphor has a limited place in finance. We must move in the direction of a solvency measure, but one uninfluenced by the lack of appetite (and weak balance sheets) of insurance companies. The question is: how much money does a closed scheme need if the trustees sterilise its liabilities and run it as a not-for-profit insurance company? This is provocative, in part because Mr Taylor lacked the time to flesh out the several ideas contained in this paragraph. But it should be obvious that the central idea is straight from the new actuaries' text book. And here he is explicit about the importance of the solvency measure as a more meaningful measure of a fund's true position.

Dealing with Permira, and facing the possibility of sponsor bankruptcy in the context of a leveraged buyout, made us more thoughtful about the risk of sponsor failure in general. Not every reader will be an expert in corporate finance, so let me translate and explain. The bid from a private-equity firm raised in the trustees' minds the possibility that the financial leverage (simply put, the company will have more debt interest to meet) involved carried with it an increased risk of failure – stretch the finances too far, and every deal will go broke. That in turn raised a disturbing question: if an acquirer can go broke, presumably so can the current owner and sponsor of our fund's liabilities. As a trustee, you might then make the leap to thinking that it is a good idea in general to minimise your exposure to the sponsor, something that can be achieved by full funding and asset liability matching.

The most crucial issue now for many companies seems to be that the pension fund deficit is itself a major source of financial instability. Trustees are being pushed into inappropriately risky investment postures in the hope that lucky market moves extinguish the deficit. It's just as likely that unlucky moves bring the sponsor to its knees. Trustees will have to understand the value-at-risk in their own funds, and the consequences of potential volatility on their sponsors' cashflow and credit rating. I could have written this myself! Actually, I wrote a less elegant and far longer version in Chapter Four.

Seventh conclusion: pension fund deficits represent a major hazard not only for beneficiaries' schemes but also for the shareholders and sponsor if the risks are not properly understood and managed.

My final conclusion is a hopeful one. For many years, companies and defined benefit pension schemes were bound together by the simple fact that employees of one were beneficiaries of the other. With so many schemes closed, that's no longer the case – 'actives' are dying out. But trustees and directors, after decades of an inappropriately cosy relationship, can with luck, understanding and firmness on the part of trustees avoid moving into the highly adversarial situation that the problem of deficits at first appears to represent. In fact, we are all in this together.

THE NEW REGIME

Insofar as Mr Taylor's speech presented a case history combined with a wish list, the latter has come much closer to reality since the arrival of the Pensions Regulator (which replaced the now defunct Occupational Pensions Regulatory Authority or OPRA). The new body's chairman, David Norgrove, is arguably the most important man in the pensions industry and one of the most important figures in the financial system thanks to his influence on corporate finance. Since he came into office on April 6th 2005, he has issued a steady stream of guidelines and guidance, and the stream is set to continue as today's proposals become tomorrow's hard manuals of best practice.

From the start Mr Norgrove adopted a simple and robust approach to the pensions problem. With rare exceptions such as WH Smith, there had been few cases of trustees actively taking on the problem of their deficit, despite ample evidence from financial economists and new actuaries of how they might do this. Mr Norgrove cut to the chase. Soon after starting in office in April he issued a 44-page "guidance" document on the rather unpromising subject of "Clearance statements". All trustees should read this document carefully, assuming they have not already done so. But it is so important that I must describe it here. You cannot be effective without knowing the vital things it says and the reactions to it.

First, the Regulator points out that under the Pensions Act of 2004, it (ie, the Regulator) is obliged to:
- Protect the benefits of members of work-based pension schemes
- Reduce the risk of situations arising that may lead to claims for compensation from the Pension Protection Fund
- Promote the good administration of work-based schemes

Right away you get the impression, then, that this is an agency that can help trustees who are determined to be effective in protecting members' interests.

"Clearance" procedures are part of the new regime. Briefly, these are (for now, optional) procedures whereby companies with pension problems (typically this means a deficit on a DB scheme) must apply for "clearance" from the Regulator for any event that might affect the pension scheme. In order to set the regime in motion, the Regulator then spelled out some basic principles, and it is these that have had the effect of dropping a large bomb on the pensions industry and on corporate finance. They are as follows:

GUIDING PRINCIPLES

General

A pension scheme in deficit should be treated in the same way as any other material unsecured creditor.

- The pension scheme is a key company stakeholder. Trustees should be given access to information and decision makers; in return they should accept confidentiality responsibilities.
- Conflicted trustees should recognise their position and act appropriately. We encourage the use of independent advice in such circumstances.
- Applications for clearance should contain concise, relevant and accurate information to enable the Regulator to reach a properly informed decision.
- All parties to clearance should act in accordance with issued guidance.
- The Regulator will wish to know about all events having a materially detrimental effect on the ability of a pension scheme to meet its liabilities.

The Pensions Regulator

- The Regulator's preferred outcome is a properly funded defined-benefit pension scheme with a solvent employer.
- The Regulator will deploy its resources in a risk-based manner.
- The Regulator will seek to strike the right balance between

reducing the risk to members' benefits and not intervening unnecessarily in the conduct of employers.
- The Regulator will be consistent in its exercise of anti-avoidance powers and the operation of clearance.

It should be obvious why this is revolutionary stuff. But just in case, go back to the first two bullet points. Just a few months ago, most sponsors would firmly have resisted the idea that a pension deficit represents an unsecured loan to them. Indeed, leading actuaries who argued as much only a year ago were accused of having gone too far. One reason is that the implication of this is quite nasty for the sponsor, especially one trying a version of "bait and switch". The Regulator makes explicit something that trustees could describe only in terms of financial theory – that the deferred wages workers receive in the form of pensions are a legally binding contract with the employer, and that a deficit therefore represents a shortfall on the proper payment schedule of those wages, such that the pension fund becomes like any other creditor who is not getting paid on time.

In fact, the idea of a firm contract was already embodied in law some time ago – it has just taken a while for many people, including trustees, to notice. Of all the dates in recent pension history, perhaps June 11th 2003 is the most significant. That was the day the Government introduced amendments to the Debt on Employer regulations enshrining the idea that companies cannot simply walk away from promises they have made to their pension schemes unless they actually go bankrupt (in which case there is now the Pension Protection Fund to pick up part of the tab). Ever since then, in part because it costs companies a lot more to shed their liabilities, trustees have been in a much stronger position.

As for the second point, this turns the employer/trustee relationship on its head. The idea that trustees have sufficient influence that the sponsor should consult them and be frank (under confidentiality) with them about its intentions is utterly novel, but utterly sensible given the pressure on trustees to close deficits. In practice, to date, I am not aware of a single company that has adopted this suggestion, although actuaries tell me that there are a very few such cases where there have been confidential discussions with trustees prior to corporate transactions – the recent deal between Ericsson and Marconi is an obvious example. However, plenty of companies are talking about it and will, almost inevitably, do so in future. Getting in the way are corporate advisers, such as investment bankers, and some shareholders who resent the change of influence and cannot understand why the mere matter of a pension deficit should hinder profit-creating deals and dividends. This tension is not to be underestimated. However, it should diminish over time as deficits are reduced and as the different parties become used to the new regime.

NOT ALL ROSES?

This is a good place to ask just how representative is the material I have cited above. You might argue that the WH Smith case was a one-off and that my extract from the reams of material put out by the Regulator is misleading because it concerns "Clearance" events, ie, those related to relatively extreme circumstances such as the impending financial weakening or even insolvency of the sponsor. These would be fair points, but they are easily explained away. It is true that not all pension fund deficits are extreme. But they all require managing, and that requires intelligent activism and persistence from trustees. In that sense, the WH Smith case is merely a precursor for many more such cases in future. It is no good sitting back and hoping that problems will disappear by themselves. As Mr Taylor said, a pension deficit is an "irregular situation that should not persist". The reason the clearance guidance is so important is that it sets a baseline from which trustees can evaluate their own situation.

This needs further explanation. Perhaps the best way trustees can tackle a deficit is to start from the worst possible outcome – insolvency of the sponsor and therefore the surety of a shortfall in the pension fund. If you can get a handle on the likelihood of the former, then you have a basis for acting to avoid the latter. And this is a spectrum. If you think your sponsor will never go bust (is it a government?) and that there will always be sufficient assets for the fund, then you can afford to be much more relaxed than if you doubt the continuity of a covenant stated today by a management that might no longer be there tomorrow. Similarly, if the sponsor has room on its balance sheet to make an acquisition, then presumably it also has room to alleviate all or part of the deficit either from cash or by borrowing. A starting point for trustees should be to ask the sponsor to explain why it is not doing so.

If you still doubt the sense of this, consider the following. Everyone uses the expression "as safe as houses", knowing that houses are not always safe. The pensions equivalent twenty years ago might have been a pension from Marks & Spencer or J Sainsbury. Who would have postulated then that the financial health of both these companies might have so deteriorated that their pension funds had become major headaches? Today we know that a giant of yesterday, even one famous for its solidity and reliability, can become a troubled and risky entity over time. It would also be wishful thinking to deny that this can happen far faster than the average forecast. The Regulator has almost gone out of his way to make this point – when things go wrong, they tend to lead to faster degradation of a financial position than anyone anticipated. And once that slippery slope has been reached, it's arguably too late for trustees to begin hand-waving. Cliff Speed points out that Turner & Newall, an early potential caller on the PPF, was once a FTSE 30 company. "The mighty can, and do, fall," he says.

It is important to remember that it is not just household names that can get into trouble so that their pension funds are compromised. There are plenty of smaller schemes that have already hit the buffers. For example, among disasters in 2004, some 200 deferred members of Blyth & Blyth's pension scheme might lose all their benefits when their scheme is wound up; members of Ilford Imaging UK's scheme were warned of massive cuts in their benefits after the sponsor went into receivership; staff in TransBus, most of whom were in the Dennis Group Pension Scheme, were expecting a severe reduction in their benefits after the scheme was reported to have a shortfall of more than £23m; and so on. (These examples are drawn from an excellent paper by Ian Greenstreet, of which more below.)

I hope this makes sense now. I think there is a direct link between the Regulator's starting point and the kind of challenge that faced the WH Smith trustee board. It's simply unrealistic to see them in isolation from each other. Indeed, we can show this by looking again at the WH Smith case, but from the company's point of view. It undoubtedly faced a tricky decision. It preferred not to capitulate to the Permira bid. But in forming its own strategic plan to put to shareholders, it must have been shocked to realise that it had to negotiate with pension fund trustees who were concerned about the implications of that plan for the future health of the fund. It must have been even more shocked to find after the event that it had paid £120m into the fund. (In that sense, ironically, Permira, far from harming the members of the fund, did it a huge favour!)

A surprising point about unsecured creditors. Did you know that unsecured creditors can apply to the courts to have a company wound up, and that the standard repayment period is 90 days? I confess that I did not know this, but in a pensions context it is rather striking. If company managers genuinely treated their pension deficits in this way, the result would be a rush to get rid of them by using any available funding. If trustees genuinely used their powers to behave like unsecured creditors, which in their case would mean winding up schemes rather than the entire company, there would be mayhem. I referred above to a paper by Ian Greenstreet. He is a lawyer and his paper addresses the question: "Should Trustees be more like Bankers?" The question has lawyerly precision. It goes right to the heart of the relationship between the sponsor and the trustees.

THE BANKING PARADIGM

Mr Greenstreet begins with the observation that pension fund issues have moved to the heart of corporate finance. There are plenty of examples, from WH Smith to Marks & Spencer, where Philip Green's £9 billion takeover bid was thwarted in part by the existence of a funding deficit in the retailer's pension fund. (Incidentally, David Norgrove, the Regulator, was chairman of the M&S trustee board at the time, so he has hands-on experience of the kind of situations his agency expects to manage in future.) Since early 2004 there has been a growing number of cases of funds that are either thwarting corporate activity because they are in deficit, or whose sponsors are threatening the PPF with default on their liabilities.

So, asks Mr Greenstreet, how do bankers act? Well, firstly, they constantly monitor the creditworthiness of their borrowers. The sponsor is the borrower of the pension scheme's money. "If a company was in financial difficulty or did not have a good credit rating a banker would either not make a loan at all, insist on additional security and/or charge a higher interest rate," points out the author. Bankers also, as a matter of course, take security for their loans. And they would probably look askance at an investment strategy heavily weighted to equities in an underfunded or mature scheme.

Until quite recently, says Mr Greenstreet, it was not common practice for trustees to monitor systematically the strength of the covenant from the sponsoring employer, and it was even less common for trustees to take security until after underfunding had been made good.

That needs to change. Trustees should actively and continually monitor the financial health of their sponsor, keeping an eye on:

- The strength of the employer's covenant/creditworthiness
- The size of the scheme relative to the employer's market value
- The maturity of the scheme, ie, the ratio of active/deferred-/pensioner members. (This is a somewhat moot point – you could argue that the split of liabilities between classes of member is much less relevant than simple solvency or lack of it.)

But monitoring is all very well. What about the power to foreclose on a loan, to call in security? Trustees lacked this power historically. Indeed, employers carried with them the implicit threat that they would terminate a scheme – something that was not too expensive under the then MFR rules.

Things have changed. "From June 11 2003 many of these considerations no longer apply," notes Mr Greenstreet (and as we noted earlier). Solvent employers now have to meet any funding shortfall on a wind-up of the scheme on an annuity buyout basis. That is so expensive that most employers would prefer to avoid it, so trustees have considerably more leverage. Thanks to June 11 and subsequent legal changes, "it is now... extremely difficult for employers to walk away from their pension liabilities".

Yes, but things remain complicated, as Mr Greenstreet shows. The remainder of his paper is full of legalese because he evaluates case law regarding the relative powers of trustees and sponsors. From September 2005 final-salary pension schemes have to meet a statutory funding objective – a requirement that they have sufficient and appropriate assets to cover their technical provisions (ie, the amount required to make provision for the schemes' liabilities). There are complex rules governing all of this, but the essence is that sponsors will have to work with trustees to make sure they are followed. Where a scheme is insufficiently funded, trustees will have to make a formal recovery plan. Again, however, exactly how this would work in practice is not yet known (see Chapter Eight for some further discussion of this). Trustees have to bear in mind that, as in other matters, their fund falls somewhere on a spectrum from fully funded with a healthy sponsor to insolvent with a near-bankrupt sponsor, and how they behave will be determined in large part by that.

The point is that although there is legal and procedural uncertainty there is also unquestionably a regime emerging in which trustees can be much more effective and indeed will have to be so if they are to carry out their legal responsibilities.

THE PROBLEM OF PRUDENCE

One of the most helpful sections in Mr Greenstreet's paper asks "Should Trustees be more prudent?" Bankers, after all, are supposed to be prudent.

There is a basic fault line in the system that administers pension schemes. Sponsors want funds to take lots of investment risk because they hope to make more investment returns and therefore pay fewer contributions. Trustees want to ensure that members' benefits are properly funded and protected as much as possible. Ironically, it is often presented that it is trustees who are being silly if they are in the business of "risk aversion". Finance directors like to assert that the sponsoring company is in the much more sensible business of "risk management", implying trustees are too conservative. But this is intellectually hollow. The worst consequences of any failure in risk-taking in the pension fund fall on the members. Proper risk management by the company would lead to full funding of the pension scheme, if necessary in combination with a share buy-back. Put more simply, if a company wants to take risk as part of its overall financial strategy, then it needs a pretty powerful explanation for why that risk should be taken in the pension fund. To date I have not found a single trustee who has heard such an argument.

New rules, including the statutory funding objective, mean that trustees are likely to be more conservative in future in their assumptions and investment strategies. According to Mr Greenstreet, "… to be prudent, trustees have to aim as a minimum in discussions with the employer (where employer agreement is required) to set contribution rates to ensure that the likelihood of surplus outweighs the risk of deficit and also to hold a proper reserve against contingencies. If agreement cannot be reached (there may be a difference of view of the degree of prudence required) Trustees should refer the matter to the Regulator for determination."

Think about that for a few moments. Have you ever had a discussion with your sponsor/employer in which it was assumed that a reasonable starting position for trustees is a greater likelihood of surplus than deficit? I certainly have not. I have canvassed a few trustees and the typical attitude they have encountered is much tougher – it boils down to a view that the trustees are jolly lucky if the sponsor offers them anything at all and that the aspiration for full funding is presumptuous, the aspiration for a surplus positively cheeky. There is a considerable gap between theory and practice.

TALKING THE TALK

An encouraging feature of the Regulator's approach is his binding in of trustees to the strategy of the sponsoring company. Regular dialogue, if necessary under a confidentiality agreement, should mean that trustees are less likely in future to have to respond to events as they unfold, but should have advance warning that a material change is coming to the table. In fact, it is hard to argue that this is anything but a splendid idea.

Unfortunately, however, dialogue is only worth something if there is sincerity on both sides, and that is something each set of trustees will have to assess for themselves. Often trustees will have to judge whether they are conducting a genuine dialogue with their sponsor or whether they have merely become part of a more sophisticated system through which the sponsor imposes its will. This will be the case at all levels. If you are trying to reduce a deficit by pressing your sponsor for more funding, it helps if you know where the company is coming from when it tells you that the lump sum of money on offer is contingent upon your accepting a lower ongoing contribution rate. Similarly, if your sponsor wants to make a big acquisition, are you really at the table, or are you just part of a rubber-stamping process?

Sadly, the only way to answer such questions will be through actual experience. It will not be easy for trustees to keep up pressure on their sponsors, not least because human nature will make it awkward. Some sponsors will push back, arguing that they cannot put more money into a pension scheme because the shareholders will be unhappy. A robust response to that is to say "So what!" and remind the company that shareholders rank behind the pension scheme in the priority list of corporate constituencies, although it takes a brave trustee board to do that. Others will argue that there is sound financial logic in running a modest deficit and taking lots of equity risk on the asset side of the scheme's balance sheet. Even if trustees have the power to override the sponsor, it will often prove difficult for them to do so in practice. It will be the case that when tensions arise, conflicts of interests will come to the fore and trustee boards will find that latent disagreements come to the surface.

What should trustees do then? Be aware of their powers and indicate that they are prepared to use them if necessary. Talk to the Regulator, who has deliberately set up systems for advice and negotiation. But stay short of actually using their powers unless there really is no alternative. The "nuclear option" for some schemes is for the trustees to order the winding up of the fund, something that most sponsors should go a long way to avoid because it, in effect, calls in the debt to the pension scheme with immediate effect. The equivalent for the company is to threaten, however subtly, closure of the scheme to new accruals. It is important that trustees with wind-up powers know how to push back, so that the sponsor is aware that the trustees know their powers and the circumstances in which they must use them.

Think back to Chapter One and the most basic issues facing a trustee, such as who your fellow trustees are and how many of them might have conflicts of interest. In this context, it is important that trustees think imaginatively about the broader conflicts within their sponsoring company. It is all very well negotiating with the chief executive, but if he is in thrall to an aggressive board of directors with strong shareholder preferences, then the trustees face an uphill battle and consequently might have to adopt a tougher attitude. Remember that the company has its own advisers (preferably independent from yours) who get paid for saying what the company wants to hear. This means there is an inherent bias – companies will always underestimate their deficits, while over-estimating future investment returns, whereas trustees will naturally tend to adopt a more conservative view.

I cannot overstate how difficult this is. The more a trustee board gets tough, the tougher it must be prepared to be if the result is stalemate or aggressive push-back. And tension will inevitably exacerbate any latent difference of opinion and practice among the trustees. Those with a normally hidden bias towards the company (whether out of loyalty or fear) might become more assertive if they are made to feel by their employer that the trustees are being unreasonable. I have heard of cases where some trustees have been labelled as "extreme" by a minority of their fellow trustees once the relationship with the sponsor became even mildly adversarial. That is not a good background against which to negotiate with a sponsor. But trustees need to ask themselves at such moments how they would feel if they had to inform pensioners that their promised benefits are not going to be honoured...

Who are your shareholders and what degree of control do they have over the board? This can make a huge difference, so ask and answer this question. It should give you a sense of where to pick your battles. If shareholders want a special dividend, then you might see that as an opportunity to ask for a meaningful one-off contribution to the pension fund. If shareholders want a steady rise in the annual dividend, then you might resist this by pressing the claim of the pension scheme to be fully funded before more money is paid out. Remember that shareholders rank below the pension scheme, even if they hate having that pointed out.

This might sound tacky, but trustees need to be prepared to think of tactics they might not have considered in the past. Why not identify and lobby key board members, especially those whose voice might be influential during a debate? At least this might give you a sense of how large the gap is between the board and the trustees. And you can also gauge the level of the board's understanding of the issues. Boards are dealing with lots of questions besides the pension fund, and they often spend only a few minutes on the topic. Like trustees, directors are under more pressure to be better informed and more hands-on, so in theory they should be learning more and asking more about the pensions issue. It is not always the case, though, and too often boards adopt a knee-jerk response to a pensions problem.

One thing trustees will have to be prepared to do, as Mr Greenstreet argues, is to refer themselves to the Regulator. Indeed, this is likely to become a common (and therefore, eventually, less confrontational) practice over time. One common referral will be over funding levels. From October 31 2005 the Regulator's guidance on funding levels sets triggers that should influence both trustees and companies, as well as a standard measure for comparison between funds. That also allows trustees to go down a new road. If you cannot agree on a funding level with your sponsor, then you can refer to the Regulator for an independent ruling. I predict that sponsors will not like this very much. But it could be quite handy for trustees who feel that their concerns are not being heard. Take the example of a fund in deficit where the trustees want full funding, but where the sponsor wants to underfund and leave a deficit that in theory should disappear five years into the future. Unless they have the power to set contributions (a power available only to a minority of trustees), most trustees have little choice but to bow to the sponsor or refer to the Regulator. There will be more and more "case law" emerging from the Regulator as the new rules bed down.

A QUESTION OF SECURITY

Back to the trustee as banker: where there is a deficit, what about the issue of security for what is an unsecured loan? Until recently, it was extremely rare for security to be either sought or offered. Further, security really needs to be given when the sponsor is in financial health – under insolvency law, it is not something that can be given to one creditor just before default to others.

There are some notable cases. One features ICI, which has a large (£6 billion) fund in relation to the market size of the sponsor (which has gradually become a smaller and smaller entity thanks to spin-offs and disposals) as well as reportedly a large deficit. According to press reports, ICI has worked with the trustees of its scheme to create a special purpose vehicle (known as an SPV) which has asset-backed guarantees for up to £250m that support the sponsor's ongoing commitments to the fund. The company is also making large annual top-up payments to reduce its deficit over a nine-year period. Too slow? Perhaps, but consider that the trustees have the security of the SPV, and their willingness to accept a slower work-out then seems more understandable, particularly because they have managed to work constructively with the employer. According to other press reports, the ICI fund has moved a big proportion of its assets into cashflow-matching bonds, away from equities. Again, trustees concerned about security of the fund have a natural interest in a more conservative approach to investment. Ian Greenstreet argues that the ICI case "arguably represents best practice" in this area. Remember the creditor's truism that "Cash is King".

That might be true, but how useful is it for most trustees? Well, if you find yourself in a similar situation to the ICI trustees and you have a willing sponsor, then fine. But most funds will face different conditions. For instance, what if their deficit is not so bad as to be on the urgent list, so that the employer simply refuses to consider granting security? Or if there is a critical deficit, but the sponsor is more inclined to flirt with the PPF (see below)? Best practice is all very well if you can make it meaningful for you. Otherwise you must do the best you can. In the short term that might mean simply raising the possibility with the sponsor and letting it permeate the overall discussion. At least that might create scope in future (preferably before things go wrong) for security to become accepted as a reasonable thing for trustees to request/demand. It also means that if there is a significant corporate event, trustees can act decisively knowing that they have already opened the discussion.

WHEN THINGS GO WRONG

One of the important ways in which the new regime is good for trustees is that things are a lot clearer when a fund hits trouble. The Regulator is taking a "risk-based" approach, as the guidance above stresses. This means that most of its resources will be focused on those funds where the sponsoring employer is closest to an insolvency that could see its pension liabilities pushed on to the Pension Protection Fund (PPF). This book is not the place for a detailed discussion of the PPF, which has already inspired reams of commentary and analysis. But I do need to spell out some basics in the unhappy event that you might find yourself in discussions with the PPF. (By the way, long before this, if you have been doing your job effectively, you will have been in discussions with the Regulator!)

The PPF will pay out a proportion of the benefits of a pension scheme in deficit in the event that its sponsor goes bust. But only a proportion: non-pensioner benefits are cut by 10%, while typically 75% of overall benefits might be paid. Also, there is a ceiling of £25,000 on the annual pension anyone can get from the PPF, which might focus the minds of a few board members!

The PPF takes an annual levy as a form of insurance premium from all company schemes. The riskier the scheme (ie, the bigger the deficit or the weaker the company sponsor) the bigger the premium, which means that a greater burden falls on the weakest funds/sponsors. That is potentially controversial, and it remains to be seen how this will bed down over time. Consistent with financial theory, there will also be a higher premium for funds deemed to be taking excessive amounts of risk, for instance by holding a very high proportion of equities. The underlying idea is a simple one: pension funds should be fully funded and should not hold risky assets. The problem is that, as in so many walks of life, there are plenty of devils in the detail. Most trustees will already see that the PPF levy raises all kinds of questions relating to the contract between the sponsor and the fund. Many of these questions are similar, if not the same, as those I have rehearsed in this chapter.

But back to the good news. There are clear rules and there is now a system that will, in effect, take over in the event of a really bad outcome for a particular fund. It should be relatively clear for trustees when their members' interests are better served by recourse to the PPF than by trying to carry on with a failing sponsor. And the Regulator's monitoring system should mean that funds with trouble on the horizon are already subject to scrutiny and help before things become terminal.

In fact the Regulator has been quite clear about how he sees his role. The more he can avoid funds becoming dependent on the PPF (and therefore drawing down the insurance), the better he will have discharged his job. The way to achieve that is to know which funds are most likely to meet trouble. And the key to that is having the right information about how well individual schemes are funded, updated as often as necessary, which is why the Regulator now has case officers focused on specific schemes or sets of schemes. Trustees who co-operate with this process should be able to show to their members that they have discharged their duties even if the outcome is a handover to the PPF.

Incidentally, under the new regime there could be growing pressure on companies to install independent trustees. An obvious reason is that they are better able to be dispassionate about the scheme and its relationship with the sponsor. Further, the worse a fund's fundamentals, the greater its need for expertise on the trustee board, something the Regulator is well placed to encourage via a network of experienced working trustees.

IT CAN BE DONE

Here, in addition to those above, are some examples of what trustees have achieved in recent years:

- HSBC recently announced an additional £1 billion paid into its pension fund in late 2005.
- In 2004, Royal Bank of Scotland paid £1.145 billion into its

pension fund, including a one-off cash payment of £750 million.

- Scottish & Newcastle made a one-off £200 million contribution that helped to reduce its deficit to around £370 million.
- Alliance & Leicester made a one-off payment of £114 million in a total payment of £152.9 million, reducing its deficit by two-thirds.
- National Grid Transco arranged for banks to provide its pension scheme with letters of credit until the next actuarial valuation in March 2007. The letters of credit can be drawn on if certain events were to imperil the interests of the scheme.
- Whitbread entered into an agreement with its trustees to pay off its deficit over a period of up to 15 years, and made undertakings to the scheme similar to some of the covenants in its banking arrangements.
- GlaxoSmithKline has made a total contribution of £1.6bn over the last three years, a net reduction in its underlying deficit of £650m, leaving the latest deficit at £1.5bn.
- Lazard paid a substantial one-off contribution into its UK pension fund from its flotation proceeds.
- Allied Domecq negotiated a £108 million payment into its pension fund as part of its takeover by Pernod Ricard of France.
- In March 2004, Marks & Spencer issued a £400 million bond and used the proceeds as a cash injection into its defined-benefit scheme.
- In October 2005, Marconi's pension fund received a £185 million cash injection, wiping out its deficit, plus a £490 million security (in the form of an interest-bearing escrow account) against future deterioration as part of the firm's takeover by Sweden's Ericsson.

Now, these cases all involve large companies with deficits. Most trustees will have to deal with smaller companies and less sophisticated discussions about how deficits can be relieved. But my point is a simple one: you can be effective and you can make a difference if you do your job properly as a trustee.

Chapter 7

ALL ABOUT ASSETS

SPEED-READ SUMMARY

- It is easy for trustees to be intimidated by investment issues because there is lots of off-putting jargon

- The biggest investment risk facing a scheme is usually its loan to the sponsor

- Most trustee boards are blinded by having the wrong investment benchmarks

- The big asset-allocation questions are relatively simple: what proportion of bonds, equities and other investments?

- The intellectual argument against pension funds as natural holders of equities has been won – equities get riskier the longer you hold them

- Put another way, equities have higher expected returns than bonds because they are riskier

- Company behaviour can be strongly driven by accounting measures that lead to policies that defy financial theory

- Trustees need to study the details of Boots' celebrated switch into bonds

- Trustees need to think more about the risks they are there to manage and the extent to which they can mitigate them using extant financial instruments

- WH Smith has been imaginative on investment as well as on trustee governance

- Betting on active fund managers is taking pot luck – there is no skill involved at all

- Trustees should ask for performance-related fees – they might just get them

Here is a true story. Shortly after I became a trustee in 2002, I attended a training course. In the afternoon there were two sessions that purported to tell trustees about the basics of investing. I confess that I found the first session pretty tedious, and was relieved when it was time for a tea break. During the break, I got talking with an older trustee who told me he sat on the trustee board of a mid-sized Midlands engineering company. He seemed a nice man, and we got talking about the mysteries of trusteeship and the session we had just endured. I said I had been bored. To my surprise, he said he was rather lost. When I asked why, he reduced his voice to a whisper and said: "To tell you the truth, I've never really understood all that investment talk. I mean, it's all jargon, isn't it. What is the difference between active and passive management, for instance? I haven't a clue." He went on to say that he sat mute in trustee meetings when investment was discussed.

That episode stayed with me. Here was a perfectly decent trustee trying to do the right thing, and he had not one clue about a major part of the trustee role. When it came to writing a book, I told myself, at least half of it would have to be a basic primer on the asset side of a pension fund's balance sheet.

The more I have looked into it, however, the more I have thought that investing is the relatively easy bit of being a trustee. In fact, as the new regulatory regime moves into higher gear, the investing bit should become even easier. That is why I propose only to walk you through the basics as I see them. I intend to focus only on the really big questions, because as I observed above there are whole libraries devoted to the practice of making money.

The biggest investment question of all for funds with a deficit is what they should do about their loan to the sponsor (since that is what a deficit is), which often represents their single biggest exposure and is a horribly concentrated form of risk.

More generally for trustees, investing boils down to just a few related issues:

- Are you investing for any reason other than to pay pensions?
- What is the right benchmark?
- What assets should the fund hold and in what proportion?
- How should the assets be managed?

Surely it can't be that simple? Well, think back to earlier chapters. Ask yourself whether there is any possibility in the present or the future that you will become a genuinely qualified investment professional. If you are on the board of a really big fund, then there tends to be a premium placed on having some in-house expertise. Really big funds often have numerous sub-committees dealing with different asset classes, for example, so they will have some trustees who develop real knowledge about, say, property or equity derivatives. But at medium-sized and smaller funds? Let's be honest, unless you happen to have a background as a trained investment adviser, then you are going to have to rely on your professional advisers. The onus on you as a trustee is not to come up with an investment strategy that shows what a genius you are at picking winners. The onus is on you to get a few big decisions right so that you can defend your choices in the future as prudent and well-informed. Especially if things go wrong.

This was brought home to me at a recent conference when a senior fund manager made a striking point. Add up the hours the typical trustee spends on investment matters each year, he said. Make a generous allowance of, say, two hours, for how much of the average meeting is spent on this aspect of the job. What is the total? If you are lucky it is one working day – about eight hours. That is not very much time given the complexity of this activity. So it almost stands to reason that it is something best left to professionals. Put another way, it is just about sufficient time to think about and discuss a few really big decisions. It is insufficient time in which to micro-manage investing in general.

The reason I say that investing will become easier under the new regulatory regime is that more and more trustees will find that they are constrained by a mixture of funding rules and regulatory requirements. This is obvious enough if you think about it. There are plenty of signals coming from the Regulator that a fund in dire straits will not be encouraged to hold 90% of its assets in equities. The PPF will look askance at this, and the trustees will find the Regulator pushing them to move to a more conservative asset allocation.

Move further back along the spectrum and even funds with deficits will find that they face penalties if they want to persist with a mismatch of assets and liabilities. Trustees will have to go with the flow, and insofar as sponsors are likely to resist, then trustees will just have to use their influence and powers. An example: many trustees, if only they read their Trust Deeds, will find that they alone have control over their investment policy. The Deed might say that the sponsor should be consulted and its wishes heard, but ultimately the trustees decide. As we have seen in earlier chapters, adopting a more conservative asset allocation can cause contributions to rise, so it is a matter that must be discussed with the sponsor. But before we get to the matter of what assets are appropriate, let's look at an absolutely basic factor that lots of trustees (and their advisers) get wrong.

BEGINNING WITH BENCHMARKS

Remember in Chapter Five we looked at the confusing way investment advisers report the performance of your fund managers? Remember, too, the point that every fund is different? Sometimes the differences are small, often they are huge. But the fact that every fund is unique ought to be sufficient for us to lay down a basic principle: the way a fund is assessed and managed should be specific to its unique characteristics. In the jargon, this is sometimes called a "scheme-specific" approach, which is just a way of making something simple sound difficult.

Notice I used the word "assessed" – it's the same as saying measured or monitored. As a matter of logic, if each fund is unique, then the right way to measure it must also be unique. Unfortunately, that is not how the pension fund industry works. Turn to your quarterly investment report and you will see all kinds of "benchmarks" cited. A typical fund might have three equity managers, a couple of bond managers, a property manager and perhaps a cash or alternative assets manager. So a typical performance report will dutifully describe each manager's performance against a range of "asset-appropriate" benchmarks. For example, the benchmark for your equity managers will normally be the FTSE 100 or 250 indexes. The measure of the manager's skill is listed in relation to the benchmark return from the index.

Think about it. What relevance does the FTSE 100 index have for your fund? None whatsoever. All it tells you is how the market has moved and therefore whether a particular manager earned above or below the market return for the relevant period. But that is not relevant to the health and progress of your fund because the market return might bear no relationship at all to your needs. What use is it to you if the FTSE 100 was down by 5% in the previous quarter and your manager was down by 4.89% when you have a £350 million deficit that also just got a lot bigger? Your manager might have "outperformed", but you have still lost a lot of money and seen the hole in your assets grow even bigger.

What would make a helpful benchmark? I mentioned in Chapter Five that some consultants have begun to introduce a performance measure that tracks the assets against liabilities, recognising that both change and that it is the relationship between them that ultimately matters. This is not a total solution for trustees, for the obvious reason that there are different ways of viewing the liabilities. Which view should you take? A wind-up measure? Some milder solvency measure? FRS17? Whatever you choose, the point is that it gives trustees a meaningful way to monitor their fund and judge when they need to intervene, either by seeking a higher level of funding or by changing the mix of assets.

GET TO THE BIG PICTURE

This has profound implications for the way funds are run. For one thing, the test of investment consultants and the fund managers they help trustees to hire is whether the overall ratio of assets to liabilities is improving, staying the same or weakening. That means there is no point in assessing a few basic points of under- or over-performance by each fund manager. Trustees need to know how their fund has really fared. Logically, the mandate to the fund manager should specify a benchmark relative to the liabilities rather than a return target relative to the market. (This would have the beneficial effect of stopping fund managers from herding around the average market return because they are all pursuing the same artificial benchmark.) This would have the added advantage of making clear that a pension scheme by definition does not want to have a year when the value of its assets falls compared with its liabilities.

An obvious objection to this is that the only place to find fund managers willing to accept this kind of return mandate is in the hedge fund industry, which has huge fees and, depending on the individual fund, may be tolerant of quite high levels of risk. All but the biggest pension funds have generally ruled out investing in hedge funds – probably correctly – mainly because they are expensive to join and tricky to monitor. The objection stands. Until trustees in large numbers start to ask for liability-based return targets (or, for instance a target return of inflation plus a set amount, or a relevant index of liabilities), then the mainstream fund managers are unlikely to offer them. Why would they? They get paid very nicely thank you for doing something much less demanding, ie, tracking the market return by a small margin of error. My point is that thinking about liability targets as a way of rethinking your approach to your benchmark is a very useful exercise.

Talk to your consultants about this issue, because it goes to the heart of your role as a trustee. Ask them what they think is the proper way for you to assess the progress of your fund. You need to take into account both the assets and the liabilities and in a way that relates them to each other. Ask the consultants if they can help to construct a new benchmark. Ask them to talk to your fund managers to explain that you are changing the way you think about their performance – at the very least you will start to make them aware that you are prepared to think logically and question the established way of doing things. After all, you ought to be asking yourself who benefits most from the established way.

THE ASSET QUESTION

It is a cliché of fund management that the really important decision facing an investor is asset allocation. What proportion of shares, bonds, cash and alternative investment (such as property and commodities) should you hold? This decision determines the bulk of your eventual returns. Fiddling around within asset classes adds only marginal value, or just as often destroys it.

Now, I have no doubt that this is true for a portfolio investor who faces no constraints – who is free to allocate assets exactly as they see fit and has the technical expertise to measure trade-offs and correlations. But let's remember that we are looking at the world through trustee-tinted lenses. There are huge constraints on pension funds. Some of these constraints are statutory – in some countries, pension funds cannot hold certain asset classes (such as junk bonds) because they are deemed by the government to be inappropriate or too risky. Some constraints are what we might call "fiduciary" – if you were to propose a particular asset allocation, say 100% in cash, you might be advised by your actuary that you would be in breach of your duty were you actually to adopt this as policy.

As well as constraints, as we have seen, pension funds also face pressures, often from their sponsoring company. The commonest pressure is to hold a large proportion of equities in the hope that these will deliver good returns and allow the sponsor to pay lower contributions both today and in the future. (We have also noted that historically this has led to the nonsense whereby the sponsor books its entirely notional profits on this deal in advance of the profits actually arriving.)

It is a fact of life that trustees spend most of the available time discussing their asset allocation. Big funds have typically evolved elaborate structures for monitoring and managing their portfolios. They have a sub-committee for this and a sub-committee for that – property, Japanese equities, Latin-American equities and so on. Even some smaller funds have surprisingly complex asset-management arrangements. Yet the trustees rarely ask themselves whether all of this effort is worthwhile. Viewed from another perspective, it amounts to pointless fiddling.

BONDS OR EQUITIES?

Anyone who has read this far will not be surprised to learn that this is the only asset-allocation question that should concern a trustee board. I would accept that there are a few huge funds which remain open to new members and which, for purposes of diversification, can make a case for holding some non-correlated assets – property, hedge funds, private equity or even art. But for the overwhelming majority of funds, the debate is clear and simple. Do not waste your time (and your transaction costs) with a multi-asset strategy. Spend the time instead becoming familiar with and then taking a decision about the debate between bonds and equities. If you do this, you can never be held by your members to have been incompetent or inadequate. (Looking back, it is the previous generation of trustees who need to answer for their unquestioning acceptance of the cult of equity.)

A brief note: there is an exception that many investment consultants might make, and which your actuary can advise as perfectly prudent depending on your circumstances. Property can be a sensible investment for pension funds, and the right kind of property has bond-like characteristics. This is something that you can debate with your advisers and fellow trustees.

Remember the phrase I quoted in Chapter Two – pensions "waddle and quack just like bonds"? It is becoming more and more accepted that because they have bond-like liabilities, pension funds should naturally invest in assets that have similar, or matching, characteristics. One helpful characteristic of bond risk is that it is often relatively easy to model and then to match – the payment or cashflow streams are predictable. So from a simple efficiency perspective, bonds are the natural matching asset class. (There are also very important tax-efficiency reasons why it makes sense for companies to make sure the pension fund holds bonds rather than equities, but these are complicated and it is really for corporate finance directors to understand them rather than the trustees.)

Yet most funds hold relatively few bonds, preferring lots of equities instead. Why? The reason boils down to what economists call "agency problems". What are they? Well, essentially they refer to situations when "agents", ie, human beings, act on behalf of "principals" – in the case of a company, the ultimate owners or beneficiaries – often in ways that defy underlying economic rationality or the interests of the principals. For some reason or set of reasons, the agents make decisions that cannot be defended on economic grounds. Managers, for example, are agents who act on behalf of company owners and, for all sorts of reasons, do things that are not at all in the owner's interests. Trustees are agents for members of pension schemes.

Let's look at an example or two, because this is an important concept. A majority shareholder who wants a company to increase its dividend might genuinely believe that money paid instead into the pension fund is wasted, even though financial theory suggests that this (if combined with some other measures) might actually create more shareholder value than a bigger dividend. The shareholder adopts the narrow view of the expected income from the investment and might therefore vote to block something that could be in all shareholders' interests.

Similarly, imagine you are the chief executive of a company with a pension deficit, but also have a group of shareholders clamouring for a special dividend. You might want to tell the shareholders to get lost while you fund the pension scheme in order to avoid an intervention by the Regulator, but you are much more likely to seek a middle path that tries to keep all sides less than furious. That "human nature" is an agency problem, because it creates a whole set of justifications for doing something that is less than efficient.

Now, multiply this kind of issue across the pensions industry. Think of how actuaries have blocked wholesale reform of their advice to customers. Think of how fund managers have insisted on benchmarks that make no sense for pension funds. Think of how consultants have been remarkably slow to pass on the lessons of a few pioneering funds so that all trustees must consider whether their alternative can still be considered prudent. The reason most funds still hold lots of equities is not because this is sensible, but because a host of agency problems has kept things that way.

Is there a case for holding any equities at all? Well, a few people think that a case can indeed be made based on portfolio theory. It is rare for bonds to match precisely a liability profile, and unless the bond holding is largely index-linked there is also a degree of inflation risk. A small proportion of equities, perhaps 10% or even, some argue, double that, might be appropriate in an effort to mitigate these risks, provided the trustees know exactly what they are doing and communicate this to their members. If you do hold equities, however, the one thing you must avoid is assuming that they will outperform when you are looking at valuation and funding. In that, at the very least, trustees need to be firm with themselves and with their sponsor.

As I write in late 2005 I think it can be argued that trustees no longer have the excuse of ignorance or poor advice if they have not begun seriously to address the bonds versus equities question. So let me explain what some of the pioneers have done and how they have justified it.

ON THE FRONTIER

Here are some facts that every trustee should already know.

In April 2000, the pension fund of Boots, the retailing and chemists chain, held roughly £2.3 billion of assets as follows: 75% equities, 20% short-term bonds and 5% cash. (The scheme, by the way, is one of the 50 largest in the UK and has more than 70,000 members.)

By July 2001, the Boots fund had sold all of its equities and short-term bonds and moved all of its assets into long-dated sterling bonds that matched as closely as possible the maturation and indexation of its pension liabilities. The bonds were held passively, with no trading and automatic reinvestment of income.

Since the Boots move, Britannic, an insurer and fund manager, has adopted the same strategy, while a few big companies such as ICI have also moved decisively (though not entirely) away from equities.

Also less well known is the story behind Boots' move. But I think it is quite instructive, not least because it shows that it is remarkably difficult to change received ways of thinking. It also sheds extremely interesting light on the conflicts and agency problems that can dominate proceedings.

The person most associated with Boots' switch, who is now an independent pensions consultant, is John Ralfe. In the mid-1990s he worked as head of corporate finance, reporting to the finance director. As he immersed himself in the company's financial structures, he began to ask all kinds of challenging questions. What would be the most efficient way for the company to structure its balance sheet? What did financial theory suggest was the best disposition of its assets?

Apart from the pension fund, the biggest issue facing Boots was its large portfolio of property leases. Mr Ralfe adopted a technical approach that viewed these as long-term liabilities (typically they have upward-only rent reviews). But they are also valuable assets, because they allow the holder to occupy and exploit space. By talking to the board and gradually winning it over to a finance theory point of view, the finance department was able to lay the ground for equally technical thinking about the pension fund. The property lease portfolio was restructured and revalued to make the balance sheet more efficient.

In 1997, several issues brought the pension issue to the fore. First, it was clear that Boots' shareholders wanted a strategic discussion with the company about the financial future: would there be a special dividend or a share buy-back to release value? The finance department began a dialogue with Boots' pension fund managers to explore how they approached investing, and with shareholders. Second, the new Labour Government abolished pension funds' dividend tax credit, which led Boots to appoint a special team to examine the implications for ongoing contribution levels. And third, the now famous paper written by Exley, Mehta & Smith was presented at the Institute of Actuaries, with all of the impact I described in Chapter Four. According to Mr Ralfe, that led lots of people, including him, to try to think through the implications.

Note that at this point I have not mentioned the trustees of the Boots fund. These included the firm's finance director and HR director, but not, importantly, Mr Ralfe. It is often assumed that he must have been a member of the trustee board and that he sat there and somehow bludgeoned his fellow trustees into changing the asset allocation. In fact, he was in an ideal position, because he could never be accused of a conflict of interest. His advice to the company and to the trustees was based on finance theory and practical logic.

Getting to the decision to sell equities was a multi-step process. After property leases (a company issue), during 1998 Mr Ralfe turned to the pension fund and began a debate on whether overall risk could be reduced by selling the fund's 5% allocation to property and buying index-linked gilts instead. This led to extensive discussions with the trustees and the fund's actuaries. It became a sort of toe in the water for the bigger question over equities.

The idea was first presented in its full form (ie, sell all equities) to the board of Boots late in 1998. It was not well received. Almost a year later, Mr Ralfe presented a less radical alternative that would reduce equity holdings to 50%, with the remainder of the portfolio to be held in long-dated bonds. To make this case, he toned down the logic of finance theory and argued more simply for an asset-liability matching idea. After this idea had been accepted by the board, there was a lengthy (and sometimes heated) debate with Boots' actuaries and investment consultants.

Finally in 2000, Mr Ralfe got the green light from the board of directors to pursue the idea of a full switch from equities. This was not without its moments. Even after the board had granted its permission, one non-executive member who had not been present tried at the next meeting to derail the move by querying the minutes and saying that had he been there he would have strongly dissented. In the end, however, the board was persuaded and Mr Ralfe was free to make his case to the trustees. Interestingly he focused his discussion with the trustees on the question of risk. "I asked them to think about what would happen to the fund were Boots to go bust," he says. "It turned out this clarified thinking on all sides." Boots began to sell its equities and by late the following year had offloaded the lot.

When Boots went public with what it had done, all hell broke loose. So here is how the trustees justified their decision:

"The move is good for Scheme members because it:

■ Significantly increases security: Matching pension assets and liabilities increases security for members, since the value of assets should always be enough to pay all pensions regardless of any movements in financial markets. This is not the case with equities.

■ Reduces costs: The management charges and dealing costs for a £2.3bn largely equity fund are significant at about 0.5% or £10m per annum. These have been reduced to £0.25m per annum.

The move is also good for The Boots Company, as sponsor of the scheme because it:

■ Reduces the Company's financial risk by matching pension assets and liabilities: Holding equities creates the risk of a deficit which would have to be met by increased Company contributions. The matched bonds move closely in line with the value of pension liabilities, drastically reducing the risk of a deficit."

Critics were rather bamboozled, to be frank, and after an initial rush of interest there was a growing silence about what Boots had done. Many trustees were advised by their actuaries and consultants that this was far too radical a step for them to contemplate, while plenty of sponsors looked at the issue and immediately looked away – why upset a generation of thinking? (On that note, there was plenty of crowing when, after Mr Ralfe's departure, a new regime at Boots moved away from the 100% bond strategy and bought some equities – look, the critics and doubters said, the strategy was always flawed and Boots has now had the courage to recognise this. Hmm. The same critics might ask why Boots nevertheless holds only a very small part of its assets in equities.)

Never underestimate the power of inertia. But that is no reason to be supine. In fact, the Boots move, because it was based so rigorously in financial theory, did act as a slow touchpaper. Very gradually, the pensions industry has been grappling with it. And equally slowly, a consensus has begun to emerge that what Boots did was right – right for members, right for management and right for shareholders.

A PERTINENT OBSERVATION

Think for a moment about the thorny issue of shareholder value. Critics of the Boots approach will argue that matching strategies using bonds are all very well for members of the pension scheme, but do nothing for shareholder value, even reduce it by forcing the employer to put more money into the scheme. If the critics are right, then logically what ought to happen whenever a fund announces that it has switched into bonds? Its share price should go down, right? What happened to the Boots share price? Absolutely nothing – it barely moved on the announcement. Similarly, on June 11 2003 when employers could no longer walk away from their pension liabilities, share prices not only did not collapse, they registered but the tiniest ripple.

Jon Exley has a nice take on the Boots case. A consequence of the change in its pension assets was that the company could no longer add around £65 million of phantom money to its annual earnings. Why? Because it could no longer pass on the presumed out-performance of the equities in the fund, as there were no longer any equities. (He calculated the £65m by applying a 4% assumed return times the 70% equity allocation times £2.3 billion.) But the share price did not react to this news. This means, presumably, that shareholders never put a value on the phantom earnings, understanding them for the accounting entries they always were. It also means that they understood the impact of the sale of the equities on the company's balance sheet as a whole. With a market value of around £6 billion, Boots sold £1.5 billion of equities, equivalent to one-quarter of the value of the company. From an investor's perspective, the company was still worth £6 billion, but it no longer had that £1.5 billion of equity exposure on its books. That made the shares less exposed to the movements in shares in general. (In technical terms, the beta of a single Boots share was reduced by about one-fifth.)

There are plenty of formal papers that explain this and the Boots affair from the perspective of corporate finance, and, as I have said above, trustees who feel they need to work through the arguments will find these helpful. Do you need to? Well, I would argue that you do if you want to understand personally the logic of moving into bonds. And if you do want to advocate a shift in asset allocation, you might well face difficulties because your fellow trustees and/or your sponsoring company do not.

PUSHING THE ENVELOPE

In the former case, you will have to decide how far you want to push the argument with your fellow trustees. You can try to get them to read up on the subject (that is something of a challenge, not least because few trustees have the time and energy to read finance theory when they have finished their day jobs, and even fewer will understand what they read). You might try opening a discussion at a trustee meeting, taking soundings around the table and making sure, as ever, that this is minuted. It is often quite revealing once you begin a process like this. If you understand something, it can be painful to listen to others spouting what you know to be nonsense, but at least you then know what you are up against. One trustee told me that on her board, the trustee who represents pensioners, ie, actual retirees, thinks it is fine for the fund to hold 60% of its assets in equities, even though it has a £400 million deficit. I'm glad I'm not a member of that fund.

My suggested route is to take initial soundings and then get your actuary and consultants involved. You can do this quite subtly by asking them for their guidance and then asking them to explain to all of the trustees how thinking has developed. For example, you might ask them simply to explain for educational purposes the reasons why Boots could justify its switch. You might ask whether your advisers have any educational materials that they can recommend to the trustees so that they can have a more informed debate in future. You might circulate to the trustee board, with copies to the finance director, HR director and chief executive, any papers that make the intellectual case for switching.

Whatever you do will have the effect of moving the debate forwards. Do not expect quick results. Boots is instructive because it took literally years of arguments and persuasion before anything happened, and even then it was quite fiercely contested. If you are starting in the Dark Ages, then Enlightenment can only come so fast.

SOFTLY, SOFTLY

The latter case is trickier. It is inherently difficult for a trustee, or even a whole board of trustees, to have a direct impact on the board of directors, unless a wholesale confrontation is underway (not recommended, unless there is no other choice). This has to be a campaign, starting with the executive management, who will have themselves to become advocates of a new approach before there will be any progress. Trustees should therefore talk to their bosses, and not be afraid to argue, to send relevant academic and industry papers, even to invite speakers to trustee meetings knowing that company representatives will be present. There is no reason why trustees should not also have lunch with board members and have an off-the-record chat/exchange of views. In fact, this can be quite useful, because it lets the board member know more about where the trustees are coming from and also opens a diplomatic door for the trustees.

All of this takes time. But I want to stress that it can all be done without causing confrontation, and you should always bear that in mind if you are feeling tempted to blow a fuse. How can you shorten the inevitable delay? My advice is to get as tough as you can with your advisers. If you haven't already, ask them some of the questions I have suggested in earlier chapters – eg, the link between assets and liabilities, is £100 of equities worth the same as £100 of bonds, etc. Ask them to recommend reading matter. Insist on their independence, so that the company becomes aware that it can no longer talk on the side to the main adviser to the trustee board. Ask them for guidance on best practice and pin them down – is there any reason why you should not embrace best practice as quickly as possible?

You will become frustrated. But if you lose your cool you will cease to be effective. There are people who want you to lose your cool, because an effective trustee can cause fundamental changes to a company's finances, and companies want to feel they are in charge of their own destinies.

OPEN AND SHUT

One firm of pensions consultants recently sent some of its clients a paper on the bond-equity issue. It was a remarkable document, but perhaps not in the way it was intended. First, there was no acknowledgement that it had taken more than four years from the announcement by Boots to the circulation of the paper admitting there is a case for bonds over equities that must be taken seriously by all stakeholders. Second, the paper concluded that the debate looks set to continue. My answer to that is that the debate is bound to continue when sensible analysts leave open the possibility that there is anything left to debate.

Now, I am well aware that there are people in high places in the pensions and investment industry who would seriously take issue over much of the above analysis – I can hear the words "tendentious", "extreme", "overstated". So let us be quite clear about the case I am making. I am writing about defined-benefit pension schemes. I am not making a more general case that it is always wrong to invest in equities. But please note, some opponents of the matched assets approach like to suggest that it makes basic mistakes about investing. And the main error that is attributed to the pro-bond camp is a misunderstanding about the nature of equity risk.

Equity risk is a subject with a huge literature. Many readers will be familiar with some of it – during the internet bubble, there was a notorious book by an American author named Jeremy Siegel called *Stocks for the Long Run*, which epitomises the view that shares become less risky if you hold them for a long period, ie, asset-allocation decisions for investors are a no-brainer. This view, assuming you accept it, is the sole justification for holding equities in a pension scheme. Pension schemes, after all, it is argued, have long-term liabilities and the cost of these can be reduced by holding equities over a very long period. Or so the dodgy accounting regimes of the past would have us think.

I think the problem is that the debate has become muddled, perhaps deliberately so on the part of the pro-equity camp. First, note that there is an important difference between something that is "long-term" and something of long duration. A pension liability is long-term in that it lasts perhaps two or three or five decades. But long-term is such an uncertain concept. Its meaning is not at all sharp. A more accurate way to describe a pension liability is as long in duration – that is a more technical finance term, but it points to the fact that the liabilities involve payments long into the future, and these can be modelled just like a long-duration bond. If you allow the use of the long-term idea, then you implicitly open the door to the argument that you should therefore endorse equities with their superior long-term returns.

Do equities have superior long-term returns? Mostly, but you pay for them. If you are really unlucky, you invested in America in 1929, or in Japan in the late 1980s, in which case you picked one of the rare periods when there was persistent equity underperformance. But the history of financial markets does support the case that equities have higher expected returns than bonds. I have already made the point that there is a reason for this – namely that equities are riskier. So the real nub of the equities/bonds debate should be whether an investor can afford to be exposed for long enough to make sure that the equity returns eventuate. Surely that makes the case for a pension fund, then, which exists for very long periods?

No. I hope I can explain this quite simply. A pension fund's primary goal is to pay members' pensions and protect their benefits in as secure a fashion as possible. Imagine, for the sake of it, a £200m fund with half of its portfolio in equities. For 30 years the fund has harvested the higher returns from equities, during which time its members gradually retire, until three-quarters of them are drawing pensions. Then in the 31st year, stockmarkets crash. The pension fund loses a big chunk of its assets. A 20% fall in the stockmarket means that £100m of equities in the fund's portfolio is now worth £80m. A 30% fall translates into an overall loss of £30m.

These are numbers than can quickly put the security of the scheme in doubt. The longer the fund holds equities, the greater the chance that there will be a significant downside event. That is not the same as saying that there will definitely be a shortfall in the fund when it is time for it to be wound up. In fact, the downside event might come sooner rather than later, and the fund might respond by becoming much more risk averse. Equities get riskier the longer they are held. (For those who are interested, the most influential writer on this is Zvi Bodie, an American academic, who has proved this using finance theory. He has also written important papers on life-cycle investing – see the list in the appendix if you want to follow this up.)

RECAST THE DEBATE

Go back to the Boots case for a moment. Recall Mr Ralfe's remarks that the trustee board got to grips with the bonds versus equities case only when it was couched in terms of risk. There is an important lesson for trustees here. You might have to accept that you are not going to win an argument about corporate finance with your finance director – the subject is too inherently tricky, because it contains the obvious subtext that the FD has not been doing his job. Similarly, the board probably will not appreciate a lecture on balance-sheet management, even if there is a huge tax gain staring it in the face.

So maybe a better way to argue the case is to do so in terms of risk. If you are isolated as a trustee, why not ask your trustee board to discuss the riskiness of your asset allocation? What is the chance that the equity portfolio will suffer from a 20% or 30% fall? How big would the deficit be in that scenario? What percentage of benefits could be paid? Will the sponsor be there with new contributions in that event?

Equally, what happens if there are good returns from equities? Will the sponsor use that as an excuse to lower contributions?

This then sets up a neat way of thinking about your asset allocation. If you hold equities, the downside risk is all in the fund because you cannot be absolutely certain that the sponsor will be there to pick up the tab at an undefined point in the future. On the other hand, the upside risk does not belong exclusively to the fund, because the sponsor can grab back some of the returns by ceasing or lowering future contributions. In normal life, people do not like propositions that have one-way downside risk and two-way upside risk. So why should trustees like them any better? (Some consultants suggest that if the sponsor wants a fund to continue taking equity risk then the trustees should ask for it to be explicit that the future returns belong entirely to the fund. My comment is that, while perfectly reasonable, this is extremely unlikely to be agreed by the sponsor.)

IT'S ALL ABOUT RISK

Risk is an increasingly useful way for trustees to think about what they do. In fact, if you go back through earlier chapters you will see that it is ever-present as a concept. I find it helpful always to bear in mind the question: what would members feel if they knew the risks being run? If the answer is that they would be to any degree shocked or perturbed, then you as a trustee should probably be doing something different. Remember that the sponsor will almost always want you to take on more risk, and will almost always offer reassurances. It is up to you to judge the meaning of such reassurances.

Once you start thinking about risk, it is quite natural to think in terms of insurance. If you fear downside risk, for example, is there a simple mechanism with which you can protect yourself? Actually, there often is, so let's explore this a little. Assume you still have 50% or 60% in equities, with no prospect of shifting that soon. Can you protect your downside? Yes, using equity derivatives. You can purchase put options that allow you to sell at a given price and so make a profit if the stockmarket falls. And it is not difficult to tailor these to pay out against set targets. If you fear the consequences of, say, a 20% fall in the stockmarket, then you can buy out-of-the-money puts that will return the equivalent of the losses on your physical holdings of shares. It is not a zero-sum deal – the put options are like a term insurance policy, so you must pay a premium, and the amount of the premium will vary depending on market conditions. At the time of writing, downside protection for a typical equity allocation might cost the equivalent of 4% of the principal being protected – not cheap, but not outrageous. If you have £100 million of equities and you want to protect against a £25 million loss, you will have to shell out £1 million. Typically, you can buy put options with a one-year maturity. So think about it. You, in effect, give up 1% of your exposure to the stockmarket in return for annual downside protection of £25 million. The cost is not negligible. But if markets do tank, they might seem very small in relation to the protection you have.

Nevertheless, this is an approach that will get more attention in future and trustees will have to learn the basics of the futures and options markets in which these transactions are conducted. One reason is that a new pension fund pioneer has emerged to challenge not just conventional, but new thinking.

IN THE NEWS

On October 13th 2005 the struggling retailer WH Smith announced its preliminary annual results. The release included a bombshell that ranks with Boots' earlier one. It read as follows:

"Non-operating activities

In September 2004, the Group completed the disposal of Hodder Headline for £224m and returned £205m to shareholders.

Following the disposal, the Group made a £120m cash contribution to the WH Smith Pension Trust. This payment was financed from the Group's own resources and new banking facilities.

In September 2005, the Trustees of the WH Smith Pension Trust adopted a new investment policy in order to limit the volatility in the underlying investment performance and reduce the risk of a significant increase in the deficit in the fund. A Liability Driven Investment approach has been adopted with 94% of the assets now invested in inflation and interest rate hedged investments (which change in value in line with changes in the underlying liabilities). The balance is in equity options designed to enable the fund to continue to benefit from any potential higher returns from the equity markets.

Following this change in the investment policy, the Board and the Trustees have agreed a new deficit funding agreement. This agreement provides the Company with greater predictability over the level of future pension deficit payments. The agreement replaces that reached last year and will result in pension deficit funding payments of £15m in 2005/06, £17m in 2006/07, £20m in 2007/08 and increasing by RPI (capped at 5%) thereafter until the deficit (as calculated under FRS17) is repaid."

Now, we have, of course, come across WH Smith before. Remember Martin Taylor's NAPF speech quoted in Chapter Six? Mr Taylor has been putting his fund's money where his mouth is. Instead of switching into bonds, it has bought a portfolio of swaps – financial instruments that allow holders of different obligations to make mutually beneficial exchanges, for example of fixed interest rates into floating rates or vice versa. And it is using equity derivatives – call options, rather than puts as in my example above – to capture what it hopes will be the upside from stockmarkets.

What on earth is this all about? What are swaps anyway? How can a fund not only largely abandon equities, but also not hold bonds? I think the relevant answer for now is that it all goes back to risk. What are the big investment risks facing a pension fund? One is changes in inflation, and another is changes in interest rates (another big risk is changing longevity, but there is not much trustees can do about that). Both have subtle, but important, effects on the value of both assets and liabilities. Broadly speaking, rising inflation is bad for bonds (except for inflation-linked bonds, but these are a tiny portion of the overall bond market), while low real interest rates raise the cost of meeting liabilities. Swaps can be used to hedge against both forms of risk, albeit at a cost. Perhaps you don't know what a swap is or how these instruments work. There are plenty of ways of finding out – see below for the reasons why you will need to in future. But as I said at the beginning of this chapter, its purpose is not to be an investment guide, but rather to call to your attention the really big issues and questions.

The WH Smith case is a striking example of emerging approaches to managing pension funds and it is one about which trustees are going to have to learn much more. WH Smith has a deficit, so its strategy must bear that in mind. But the strategy is not a risk-averse one. By shedding unwanted elements of risk, the trustees are trying to target more precisely those risks they do want to take. And they are doing so in full consultation and collaboration with the sponsoring company, with the shared underlying motivation that neither party wanted a deficit in future that would require a big cash contribution. Such strategies come from a new part of the pensions market – capital-markets specialists, mostly the big investment banks that know how complex hedging and derivative instruments work. And they are selling an interesting idea – that of "de-risking" pension funds.

WAKING UP TO LDI

As I have remarked, this book cannot be a comprehensive guide to the many investment issues facing trustees. But I need to spell some things out clearly. Because it is the subject of growing discussion, it is vital that trustees begin to become familiar with Liability Driven Investment or LDI, as it is called. (LDI is an acronym that will become as familiar to trustees as RIP.)

If you want to reduce the risks facing a defined-benefit pension fund, you must accept a few things that are not immediately obvious. The biggest one is that there is a price to be paid for reducing future uncertainty. It is prohibitively expensive to reduce risk entirely, so the idea behind LDI is to lessen the cost by focusing on some of the big risks and narrowing the range of possible future outcomes. A narrow definition of LDI would be to call it a hedging programme that zaps the negative effects of the biggest financial risks facing a fund, namely interest rate risk and inflation risk. (The analogy is slightly misleading because true hedging is, in effect, an overlay – it sits on top of or alongside existing structures, so that the investor remains exposed to the volatility of those structures.) Another way of looking at this is to say that a fund gives up some of its upside returns in order to limit its exposure to the downside, because the consequences of the latter are so much more painful than those of the former.

That is the theory. The practice is horridly complicated. In fact, it involves financial engineering so tricky that only a tiny minority of trustees are likely to understand it in detail unless they embark on some serious education. Do you know what a swap is, let alone a swap curve? How much do you think you should pay for a swap? And how much do you know about call options? It is likely, almost certain, that in subsequent editions of this book I will have to explain such things in much more detail. Today, however, most trustees are only just beginning to hear about LDI, so it is more important to introduce the concept than to give it a full exegesis. (Look at the websites of some of the leading investment banks, several of which offer primers on swaps, although be warned – they are quite complicated, and you are likely to get fairly garbled explanations from actuaries who themselves are struggling to learn about all of this.)

BACK TO RISK AGAIN

Trustees also have to understand that LDI does not mean that a fund ceases to have any risk. The only way to get rid of all risk is to trigger buyout and then cashflow match until the fund expires. If you do undertake an LDI programme, it is important that you understand the residual risks and what you would do if things go wrong. One helpful way to think about this is to ask how you would explain your decisions to the trustees who will succeed you in future. Will they thank you or curse you?

LDI is both a danger and an opportunity for trustees. Sophisticated investment banks are not entering the market out of the goodness of their hearts. They spy an opportunity to create new demand for their products, deepening liquidity and market efficiency while also making a profit. Trustees need to be exceptionally careful that they understand these products and exactly why they might want to use them. As ever, they will need to be able to explain clearly to their members what they are doing and why, just as they should if they are following a "conventional" strategy.

I go back to something I have said over and over in this book. Ask your advisers. Get them to explain. And then discuss it with your fellow trustees. Is this for you? Is your fund big enough to justify the transaction costs? Is it the right approach to risk management? What could go wrong? What would be the consequences of things going wrong? What does your sponsor think?

At this point, let's take stock. Notice that you have been reading for quite a while on the subject of investments or the asset side of your role. Yet I have hardly talked at all about the kinds of things covered in most materials relating to this area. No lengthy discussion of portfolio theory. No explanation of alpha or beta. Only the briefest description of different asset classes. Can this be right?

It can. But perhaps I should reiterate what amounts to a mild warning to trustees. You will have to get up to some speed, if not full acceleration, on issues such as LDI, because increasingly you will be judged by new standards set by both the Regulator and the marketplace. If a fund, or several funds, have successfully undertaken LDI-type strategies and explained them in sensible terms to members, then that sets a new benchmark for your behaviour and you will be required to examine your past and present decisions. There is plenty of available training on this and there are regular conferences on LDI strategies, and it's always worth checking whether, as a trustee, you can attend at no charge – often the banks and consulting firms are picking up most of the tab in the hope that more trustees will attend and begin to understand the new concepts.

Remember that ultimately the challenge is to be effective. Even if you can't be an expert, at least you can behave judiciously and get the most out of your advisers. Nowhere is this more the case than in the issue with which I opened this chapter – what on earth is active investing, how does it differ from passive investing, and which one is better for pension funds?

ACTIVE OR PASSIVE?

Of course, the difference between active and passive management is easy enough. Active managers take bets that they hope will allow them to perform better than the market – ie, they invest differently from the market as a whole, because they believe they know their stocks better than the market on average. Passive managers create portfolios that precisely mimic the market as a whole and therefore produce (within a tiny margin of error) the market return. Often these portfolios are designed precisely to match a stockmarket index, which is why passive management is also referred to as "indexation".

One feature of active investing that is poorly understood is that it is a zero-sum game, albeit a lucrative one for the fund managers who gather investors' fees. The simple explanation is that there is an overall amount of return in the market. As a matter of logic, not all of the active managers can do better than the market – some will, some will inadvertently match the market, and others will return less than the market so that they offset the extra returns of the successful managers. If somebody does better than the average, there has to be someone somewhere else doing worse! Put another way, successful active managers are merely eating the lunch of those unsuccessful active managers. Actually, as Peter Tompkins of PricewaterhouseCoopers points out, fund managers, whether successful or unsuccessful, are all eating lunches paid for by us!

Now, the question for trustees is a simple one: should you pick active managers and hope they outperform? Or should you seek only the market returns and opt for a passive strategy?

How should you think about this problem? One factor that it is important not to overlook is that active managers charge more for the skills they try to deploy. Depending on how trendy their skills are (and how many trustees were persuaded into so-called "high alpha" funds in recent years?) the managers can charge juicy fees – perhaps 1% of assets annually or sometimes more. True, this makes hedge funds look cheap, but that is my point. By contrast, passive managers charge far less, on the grounds that they merely construct and then tweak market-matching portfolios. They do not do any of the clever screening and stock-picking that characterise active strategies, although some of them offer so-called "enhanced indexation" where they use clever techniques to try modestly to outperform the index (for example, by anticipating which shares are set to move in and out of the index). A fee for a typical index fund can be 0.0125% of assets. A big difference. Remember how much Boots saved by changing its investment strategy?

COSTLY ACTIVITY

On costs grounds, then, passive management and the market return looks a winner. But what about the possibility that a brilliant active manager will produce such amazing returns that they more than justify the fees? A typical active mandate will specify something like "index plus two percentage points" as the target return. This means that in a year when the market is up by 10%, the active manager should be up by 12%. If the return is less than this, the manager has failed to fulfil its mandate. But it will still be paid. Performance-related fees are still unusual, at least in the UK market. So you run the risk, as trustees, of earning the market return or less, but paying high fees for this when you could have paid index fees. Explain that to members.

Further, what strikes you about that 2%? It strikes me that it is not very much by way of upside. At least hedge funds tout 20% or 40% returns – of an order that, if you were to get lucky, would make a tangible difference to the health of your fund. But 2% upside, unless it could be repeated reliably year in, year out, seems like small potatoes to me. And we know, because finance theory tells us so, that active managers follow a "random walk". They do not know from one year to the next whether they will outperform. They hope they will, and survivorship bias (ie, failing funds are closed down and disappear from the statistics) means that there are always a few firms that can boast uninterrupted long-term records. But there are no guarantees, and there is always a chance that trustees will pick a manager just as its form dips.

In essence, then, trustees must think through the following questions:

- Do they want to hire active managers and in what terms will they explain this decision to members?
- For what proportion of their assets?
- Do the higher fees justify the promise of higher returns?
- Have the trustees asked for a performance-related fee, so that they can explain this to scheme members?
- Have they asked their actuary to model the impact on the fund after five years and ten years if the managers perform as they have promised?
- Are fees and performance for an active manager measured relative to those of a passive manager?
- How much underperformance will they tolerate before they fire a manager?

The last question is a tricky one. If you ask a typical trustee what he or she thinks are the big investment-related issues they face, you are unlikely to get as an answer the decision to fire a fund manager. Trustees are quite reluctant to fire managers, and the reason goes back to the agency problems I discussed above. If you have appointed someone full of hope that they will deliver, you will tend to give them extra time if the expected performance is not there. The analogy might be with you making a direct investment and hanging on to it even long after it had gone nowhere.

PAY FOR PERFORMANCE

In fact, trustees ought to be much more ruthless with fund managers, both in demanding lower fees and performance guarantees and in being prepared to fire them quickly. I have heard of several egregious cases where trustees clearly felt powerless or embarrassed to confront an underperforming manager, even though it was obvious that things had gone wrong. In one case, a manager successfully offered the explanation that one-off administrative errors had caused a period of poor performance, and the trustees did not even ask for a refund! In another case, a fund manager closing a poor fund insisted that the customer had to pay the fees for switching into an alternative fund.

I think it helps to recall the mantra: "Try explaining that to members!" Follow the logic. In any other walk of life if a service provider screws up they pay you back what they have lost. In fund management, it seems, it is always the customers who pay. This has to be largely the customers' fault.

Chapter 8

LOOSE, BUT IMPORTANT, ENDS

SPEED-READ SUMMARY

- Trustees must understand that their role is hugely influenced by agency problems that are extremely difficult to overcome

- Funds will face more and more questions about whether their specific policies on transfer values and commutation factors are fair to members

- The Regulator's work on scheme-specific funding is vital for trustees, so they must read it and make sure they have understood its implications

- The idea of a partnership between trustees and the sponsoring employer is built in to the Regulator's assumptions, but in practice it can be tricky to have a genuine partnership

- The Regulator's Guidance on funding includes some of the best available advice for trustees, not least its reminder of the basic principles of the job

- If trustees make a better job of being effective, then they can make a real difference to the future for their scheme members

Remember in Chapter Two I explained some theory about pension funds based on work by, among others, Jon Exley. I have left it right until the end of the book to explore briefly the next step in his argument. Having set out why defined-benefit pension schemes exist, Mr Exley asked the question: how should they be managed?

The purist's answer is that pensions should be bought through an insurance provider. But if they are offered by a company, then, says Mr Exley:

- The plan should have a matching (100% bonds) investment strategy
- The plan should be fully funded

He goes on to say, "The reasons for these conclusions are very well rehearsed in the finance literature." This is certainly true. As I have already said, there are yards of books that rehearse and re-rehearse these arguments. Given all of the other analyses in this book, and in the handful of papers referenced in the appendix, I don't think it is necessary to spell out all of the arguments here. The amazing thing is how and why the pensions industry has lagged so far in practice behind the theory. How do we explain that?

The main answer is agency issues of the type described in the previous chapter. Mr Exley has done excellent work on this and I think it is worth a quick look at his analysis. Remember the idea that owners and shareholders are principals, and managers are their agents, and that these groups can occasionally come into conflict? Well, think about it in terms of a pension fund. The deliberate mis-matching of assets and liabilities in a pension fund has an effect on a company's overall balance sheet – in effect, it raises the firm's gearing (more equity, fewer bonds). That creates delicate agency issues, because, as Mr Exley points out, the effects of the gearing are not symmetric. If a deficit emerges, then managers can call on shareholders to make it good. However, a surplus tends to stay largely in management hands in the form of greater free cashflow. "Systematic under-funding of schemes can give company management access to substantial amounts of cash," writes Mr Exley.

It is also arguable that pensions where a scheme is deliberately mismatched are an inefficient form of remuneration – the only reason employees accept them is because they have not been offered much of a choice. It is almost impossible for members to assess accurately the employer's intention to restore a deficit. By contrast, where a scheme is fully funded and invested in matched assets, then there is a transparent and easily valued benefit (because it can be priced against the equivalent available insurance contract). There are also management costs from mismatching, a fact that more and more managers will be aware of now that they must operate under the new regulatory umbrella.

One of Mr Exley's most powerful weapons in addition to razor-sharp analysis is humour. He points out that opponents of full funding and liability matching often adopt positions that require tortuous and contradictory reasoning. For instance:

- Pension funds should invest in equities when they have the "cushion" of a surplus. Pension funds should invest in equities in order to extricate themselves from a deficit.
- Equities match liabilities in the long term, but also generate short-term surpluses that can be spent by reducing contributions.
- It is beneficial to invest in equities and underfund a plan, despite the fact that this leaves the tax benefits of full funding and bond investment grossly underutilised.
- It is in shareholders' interests to underfund a pension scheme because there is an implicit option to default which has a value. But pension schemes are an essential element of a paternalistic employment model.
- Deferred annuities provided by insurers are very expensive, but the annuity market remains small because of the extremely low return on capital achieved by insurers.

And so on. It is a measure of the task facing trustees that there should be such intellectual confusion. It takes a certain confidence for trustees to see their way through this to a clear set of policies and ideas. But the good news is that this is getting easier. As we saw in Chapter Six, there are more and more examples where funds have defied the old wisdom and yet the share price of the sponsoring company has not collapsed. And, as I have said many times, the new regulatory regime, by clarifying guidance and setting new standards and trigger points for schemes, is a blessing (as well as a burden, of course!).

ELEPHANTS IN THE ROOM

In the last few pages I will discuss scheme funding and explain the approach adopted by the Regulator. This is essential reading for all trustees who want to be effective. But before we get there, there are a couple of issues that fall into what we might call LDI territory – by that I mean they are big, getting bigger and are poorly understood and explained by both trustees and their advisers. They are commutation factors and transfer values.

First, read your Trust Deed, as I urged in Chapter Three. You almost certainly have powers over both these factors. Both are technical, especially commutation because it involves tax. But ask your advisers, especially your scheme actuary, to explain the assumptions that are being applied. In the case of transfer values, for example, many funds have adopted a punitive approach designed to discourage members from transferring their assets if they leave the company. Is that fair? Surely someone deserves a decent value for their assets? How are values set by your fund? Using what rates of return? You could argue that it is in the interests of the scheme and the sponsor to offload any liabilities they can if the cost is less than the buyout value. So a fair transfer system would pitch transfers generously but below buyout. Leavers could then decide for themselves whether to take the deal or leave their assets in the fund. (The Institute of Actuaries is currently looking at new guidance on this issue, so expect it to become an agenda item soon.)

Ditto commutation factors – some schemes, encouraged by their advisers, but probably because the trustees do not understand the importance of the issue, are offering lousy rates to members who want to take cash lump sums instead of pension when they retire. Remember that trustees need to watch over the interests of all members. Again, ask your advisers and do something – there is no excuse for not taking action.

A QUESTION OF FUNDING

One vital element of the blessing is that the Regulator has set out how trustees must operate when their scheme has a deficit to a level of detail that is unprecedented. At the time of writing, the Regulator had just issued his consultation document on scheme funding, a 90-page tome that can be found at: www.thepensionsregulator.gov.uk/pdf/schemeFundingConsultation. pdf. By the time this book has been published, it is likely that the consultation will be over and the Regulator will have released the formal statement of powers that is set to follow. It is possible there might be some delay as the company lobby tries to get the funding rules watered down, but the final document will be one of the most important things for trustees to read in full (along with their Trust Deeds and rules).

I hate to insist on the reading of any official tome, let alone a 90-page one, so let me explain why I think this particular document is so crucial. All trustees will have to become familiar with the "trigger" system the Regulator is adopting to monitor and track pension funds. Indeed, the Regulator goes out of his way in the consultation document to point out that "Trustees have a key role in relation to scheme funding, because of their fiduciary duties to scheme members and because of their legislative responsibilities. From April 2006 trustees must have knowledge and understanding of (amongst other things) the principles related to the funding of occupational pension schemes."

Now, look carefully at that statement. It suggests a rather different approach from the one I described in Chapter Two. There I suggested that trustees should not panic because so long as they have collective expertise they should meet the Regulator's requirements. That is less clear now. I attended a conference in November 2005 at which a senior actuary working for the Regulator argued that every single trustee will have to meet the knowledge and understanding benchmark. An obvious conclusion is that trustees are going to have to undertake a lot more training in the coming months and years. The stipulation I have quoted comes from Chapter Seven of the consultation document, and it is a pretty sharp call to trustees to realise that they have an absolutely essential role to play in future.

The chapter goes on to explain:

"Trustees are responsible, under the new legislation in Part 3 of the Pensions Act 2004, for decisions on scheme funding. After taking advice from their actuary and usually with the agreement of the employer, trustees are required to choose prudent actuarial assumptions to be used in the calculation of the scheme's funding target. If that target is not currently met, the trustees must decide how and when to meet it in a way that is appropriate to the specific circumstances of their scheme."

And if you cannot agree with the employer? Again, the Regulator is clear that it will intervene, sometimes even when it has not been asked to do so. And here's the rub for trustees. It's no good sitting back and waiting for the Regulator to come to your rescue. That won't wash at all, because the Regulator is going to expect to see that you have been doing your job properly. You might be asked for documentation to prove that you have conducted your affairs properly and handled discussions with the employer fairly and effectively. The Regulator will not assume that only the sponsoring company is capable of behaving unreasonably. So he is raising the bar for trustees as well as for sponsors.

AN INTERESTING PARTNERSHIP

Let's go back to the earlier point, for a moment. The new funding regime in Part 3 of the Pensions Act 2004 is based on a partnership approach between the trustees and the sponsoring company. Its main features are that:

- Every scheme must have regular funding valuations at no more than three-yearly intervals
- Every scheme must adopt a funding target (the technical provisions) specific to the circumstances of the scheme on actuarial principles to make provision for benefits already accrued
- Trustees must obtain the employer's agreement to the method and assumptions for the calculation of technical provisions where valuations reveal a shortfall (assets less than funding target)
- Trustees and employer must agree a recovery plan to eliminate it
- Future contributions from members and the employer, including

those to implement any recovery plan needed, must be set out in a schedule of contributions agreed with the employer
- Trustees may agree with the employer to reduce future benefit accrual if agreement on funding cannot otherwise be reached
- Failures to complete any element of the scheme-funding process within legislative timescales must be reported to the Regulator
- Trustees may only make funding decisions after obtaining actuarial advice

Clearly it is important for all trustees to make sure that they familiarise themselves with these new rules and procedures. The principles for being effective, however, have not changed. Get the cash you need to protect members' accrued benefits and keep it safe from erosion. Do you have the money you need to pay the pensions promised? Are you getting enough money in for the new pensions being promised? If you can answer yes to these questions, then you are doing your job as a trustee. Admirably. If not, then you must act.

The Regulator also sets out what he sees as the biggest risks associated with scheme funding. These are as follows (from page 26 of the Consultation document):

- That the employer goes out of business leading to scheme wind-up while there are insufficient funds to meet the pension promise to scheme members. Where the funds cannot even meet the level of benefits protected by the PPF, the scheme may enter the PPF and members will receive benefits, but only up to PPF levels
- The trustees set technical provisions at too low a level to discharge their responsibilities given the circumstances of the scheme, for instance because the investment return achieved is less than that assumed in the calculation of technical provisions
- The trustees agree to such a long recovery plan that there is a real possibility that the employer will cease to be able to find the necessary funding during that period
- The trustees or employer abdicate their responsibilities and leave the Regulator to become the arbiter or standard-setter for scheme funding – we were never positioned to perform this role
- The expenses incurred are more than that assumed in the

calculation of technical provisions, for example an increase in the PPF levy because more schemes enter the PPF than expected

This might not look like it, but I think this sounds a warning bell for trustees. It suggests that there is a level of technical expertise required in the discharge of trustees' duties that has probably been rather neglected to date. Ask yourself, for example, if you can say with confidence that your technical provisions are set at the right level. My guess is that you don't even know what they are or what this means.

BACK TO BASICS

I'm going to give one final extract from the document to demonstrate that trustees absolutely must read it. On page 28, the Regulator sets out the principles that underpin his approach to scheme funding. They are:

- **Protecting members** – employers should aim to keep promises to pay benefits from pension schemes at the level that members are expecting. This means that schemes should aim to be funded so that they can pay all benefits promised to members as they fall due, bearing in mind the risks that investments may under-perform or liabilities increase over time.
- **Scheme specific** – each scheme needs to take account of its particular circumstances, because there is no standard funding formula. Trustees should take into account not just the risks specific to the scheme's assets and liabilities but also the risk that the employer may cease to be able to support the scheme at some stage in the future.
- **Risk-based** – regulatory intervention should be focused on the schemes that pose the greatest risk to their members and the PPF. Neither the Regulator nor anyone else can eliminate all risk. But we will seek to mitigate those risks that can be identified and will focus on the schemes presenting the most serious risks. ... underfunding varies considerably between schemes. There are similarly large variations between the risk of employers becoming insolvent. And there are large variations in the size of schemes. Our focus has to be on those schemes where the risk to members and the PPF is greatest.
- **Proportionate** – trustees are required to correct any shortfall as

quickly as the employer can reasonably afford. This means that we should treat differently those schemes where rapid elimination of the shortfall would have a serious impact on the employer and those where employers could potentially afford to pay off the shortfall more quickly.

- **Preventive** – we need wherever possible to act before risks materialise. Relatively small changes in some assumptions can have a significant effect on liability values and hence on funding requirements. If inappropriate technical provisions or the recovery plan are not challenged then a subsequent employer insolvency will leave the scheme in a more exposed position than might otherwise have been the case. The scope for effective intervention is much reduced once this happens.
- **Practicable** – we need an approach that can be operated within the constraints of the information and resources available to us, and to minimise additional burdens on schemes. The approach also needs to be operable in a way that is demonstrably consistent in similar circumstances.
- **Referee not player** – trustees and employers with the help of their advisers must ensure that schemes are fully funded. It is not our role to interfere with that responsibility where it is discharged consistently with their own duties.

These consultation proposals on funding followed an earlier "Guidance" document issued by the Regulator in March 2005. This deals specifically with the funding of defined benefits and contains some useful summaries of the way trustees can approach funding issues. For example, many trustees will not be familiar with the precise order in which the elements of a funding exercise should be done. Thus, says the Regulator, it might be as follows:

- Statement of funding principles
- Technical provisions – methods and assumptions
- Actuarial valuation
- Recovery plan (if needed)
- Schedule of contributions
- Repeat process until agreement is reached (including considering modifying future accrual of benefits if appropriate); then obtain
- Certification of the schedule of contributions

The Guidance then goes on to set out how trustees can meet the "key obligations" under the process. This part of the report, which begins on page 10 and runs until page 18, is extremely useful. I am not going to simply copy it out here or paraphrase it. Suffice to say it explains quite clearly some tricky subjects, notably different ways of calculating technical provisions and deciding which method is most suitable for your fund (remember that funding is on a scheme-specific basis, so there is no blanket solution). I think we are in what I call "Trust Deed territory" here. By this I mean that this is a document that every trustee should read and try hard to understand. It takes only a few seconds to locate the document and the more recent consultation paper, and they can be read and digested in a couple of hours. I urge you to do so.

If in doubt about the meaning of some of the more technical issues, ask your advisers, having first made sure that they are independent of the sponsoring company. And go on asking until you genuinely understand the issues and are able to make informed decisions. If you can't, or are not prepared to put the effort in, then you should resign. But before you do that, ask your company for time off so that you can have some peace and quiet in which to get to grips with the job and how it is changing. No reasonable employer will refuse.

HALF FULL, HALF EMPTY

It is worth saying again that it can feel a thankless task being a trustee. You might achieve a big degree of safety for members' existing benefits, only to find they are furious with you when future benefits are cut. You might struggle on a conflicted trustee board and then be blamed for not fighting harder to get things changed. You might be unable to shift your fellow trustees to a more rational investment strategy, and unless you actively dissent using the official minutes, you will take the rap if things go wrong.

More positively, however, in each of the above cases you have given cause for members to be extremely grateful, if only they know what is going on. Make sure they do know. This does not mean breaking confidentiality. But be sensible about when you can and cannot tell members what is going on. Often communication can be the best way to defuse potential tensions. It can help you as a trustee to know that there are people rooting for you. And it can provide tangible proof of my single most important point: you can be an effective trustee. It's just a matter of knowing a little and asking a lot.

Perhaps unsurprisingly, commentators were quick to seize upon the Regulator's funding proposals and point out that the whole new pensions edifice depends to an unprecedented degree on the effectiveness of trustees. As the *Financial Times* pointed out in an editorial on November 2 2005, "the new system will live or die by their ability to make finely nuanced judgments and avoid either kowtowing to management or insisting on crude rules of thumb. The £76 billion question is: are they fit for the task?" I think that they are. But they will need to be at the top of their game.

ALL YOU NEED TO KNOW ABOUT BEING A PENSION FUND TRUSTEE

AN INTERVIEW
WITH DAVID NORGROVE
(October 2005)

Q: How do you view the origins of today's pensions crisis?

A: I don't know if it's a crisis – it's certainly not like a banking crisis. But it is a serious issue, socially and economically. I think you have to go back to the origins of DB schemes and remember that insolvency is a random walk – that combined with too much equity, meant that there was probably much more risk for members than people were aware of. The scale of the problem has gradually become clearer as governments have tightened the rules governing schemes. And, of course, the problem has been compounded by low real interest rates and rising longevity.

Q: How bad is the deficit problem?

A: Frankly, the numbers are all over the place. There are something in the region of 9,000–10,000 DB schemes, but thanks to calculations made on widely differing bases, plus huge uncertainty around longevity, it's impossible to put a meaningful number on things. We're in the process of getting standardised information on all funds that will allow us to evaluate the deficits and how assets are being deployed.

Q: How have you approached the job?

A: The immediate focus has been on Clearance, partly for obvious reasons such as protecting the Pension Protection Fund against moral hazard. The guidance is designed to create clarity around corporate transactions. In some ways, it's an odd role for a government regulator, because in many cases we are required to confirm that we will not use our powers. But the principles are clear enough. We only want approaches if there is likely to be a material effect on a pension scheme, and we have defined these situations, for example a change of control.

Q: *Have you had many approaches?*

A: So far we have had around 270, only one or two of which have been refused, though in most cases there has been a change in the transaction or the position of the pension scheme. By the way, Clearance episodes are exempt from the Freedom of Information Act, for obvious reasons.

Q: *Can you explain the idea of pension funds as creditors?*

A: Well, we see pension schemes with deficits as unsecured creditors, but that is because this approach is statutory – it's embodied in the Pensions Act. Ultimately it's about making sure that pension deficits and liabilities are transparent and are built into shareholder expectations. Certain bad news is much better than uncertain bad news.

Q: *What is the thinking behind the new funding regime?*

A: You need a little history here. Despite good intentions, the MFR proved to be inflexible to changing circumstances and ended up being pitched too low. It was viewed by the Treasury as distorting investment decisions. It is therefore being abolished. At the same time, the European Directive on pensions was looking at funding and toyed with the Dutch model of 104% of buyout, before settling on saying that schemes should be fully funded to be meet their liabilities as they fall due, with a concrete and realisable recovery plan where this is not the case. That was translated into the Pensions Act such that specific schemes must have a funding target based on prudent assumptions and a recovery plan setting out when that target is to be achieved. From our perspective as a new regulatory body we felt there was a need to try to define how we would determine which schemes might not be applying these requirements in a way that protects members' benefits and reduces risk to the PPF.

Q: *How did you frame the issue?*

A: There are two main areas where we will be involved. First, where there is no agreement between trustees of schemes and the sponsoring company we will be required to set funding targets and recovery plans. Second, the data we are gathering will allow us to assess where the risks really are. To do that we need to set filters or triggers to pull out the schemes that will need a further look. We've proposed two triggers for consultation. The first combines FRS17 with the cost of buying PPF benefits – it looks as though on average these are both roughly the same as 75% of full buyout costs, although there are quite wide variations. In other words, a scheme with a funding target below FRS17 or the PPF minimum may well attract our attention, those above may well not. Then we have looked at recovery plans and assessed how quick they should be. At one extreme, if the money is there, why not pay it to the scheme? At another, a company will struggle to pay, and there is no benefit to anyone in driving it into bankruptcy. We will be flexible around a trigger of ten years. The essence, then, is to look at schemes in terms of their specific circumstances, including their maturity, and the covenant of the employer for example.

Q: *Can DB schemes survive?*

A: There might be a faster end to new accruals. I'm reasonably confident that in the majority of cases, barring a really unforeseen catastrophe, we can turn the ship around. The new mark-to-market focus means you cannot make heroic return assumptions. But the employer covenant, not investment return assumptions, is the biggest risk facing any scheme.

AFTERWORD & BIBLIOGRAPHY

In Chapter Five I discussed the idea that for trustees trying to assess their fund it can be a bit like trying to hit a moving target. It was somewhat like that writing this book – every week, almost every day, something would be announced that added a detail or moved the subject on a little (sometimes a lot). For instance, the same day I was writing this brief conclusion just before going to press, the Co-op announced the closure of its defined-benefit scheme, joining the small, but growing ranks of companies who have decided to abandon the final-salary retirement benefit.

I suppose there was something especially symbolic about this move by a group that has a relatively unusual form of social contract with both its workers and its customers. I do not know anything of the inside story, but it seems a safe prediction that where the Co-op goes, others will not hesitate to follow. Indeed, Arcadia, Philip Green's retailing group, announced to staff that they would have to work longer and pay higher contributions in order to earn their pensions. A week earlier Rentokil Initial closed its DB scheme to all further accruals. And so on. And on. In the end I simply had to decide to call a halt and get the book published. Any changes can await the next edition.

In light of these recent events, my message to trustees is that they should not be too daunted. You cannot stop your sponsor from altering the rules of the game in future. But you can and must use your powers responsibly and forcefully to claim and protect what already belongs to you and your members. If you do that, then you must know all you need to know about being a trustee.

A WORD ON SOURCES

As you will have read, some web and article references are scattered through the text in the chapters above. It is not my intention to write a full bibliography, as the purpose of this book is more to point trustees in directions they can go if they wish to learn more.

It might help trustees who feel relatively exposed about finance and investing to read a couple of general books. One excellent book is by Peter Bernstein. *Against the Gods* tells the remarkable story of risk, but in a lively and fascinating way. My own earlier book, co-written with Ron Dembo, is a shorter introduction to risk: *Seeing Tomorrow: rewriting the rules of risk*, was published by Wiley in 1998 and focuses on introducing downside risk and specifically the concept of "regret" into decision-making. Like this book it is meant to be accessible and useful.

Most of the more specifically relevant papers and articles are available on the web, and a bit of diligent searching can take you a long way. For example, it is easy to find the main papers by, say, Jon Exley, simply by a name search with the word "pension" or "pensions" added. Ditto if you are trying to find an influential paper by, say, Charles Cowling. The key 1997 paper, by the way is:

"The financial theory of defined benefit pension schemes" by CJ Exley, SJB Mehta & AD Smith, presented to the Institute of Actuaries, 28 April 1997.

Here is some more specific advice, however. There is a host of articles and thoughtful papers on the website of GEMS, or the Group for Economic and Market Value Based Studies, a resource put together by Mr Exley and his co-authors:

www.gemstudy.com/index.htm

The DB and DC parts of this site are especially helpful, and it is worth looking at the links too, particularly those to the sites of Jeremy Gold, an influential American thinker on actuarial and pension matters, and John Ralfe, mentioned above in the context of his work at Boots and his subsequent role as a consultant. Both sites have really useful content, but also invaluable additional links. If you are interested in the equivalent debate, say, on actuaries in America, then these are good routes to follow.

Among the more indispensable names to explore:

- Zvi Bodie and his concept of life-cycle investing as well as his work on long-term equity investment
- Jon Exley – pretty much all of his published work
- Charles Cowling and co-authors on scheme funding, but also on pretty much everything
- Cliff Speed, especially recent work on trustees as bankers

Each of these names will open further avenues for you to explore should it interest you beyond the scope of being an effective trustee.

Finally, it is too early for me to have formed a view, but the Regulator has now posted the beginnings of his promised e-learning service for trustees at:

www.thepensionsregulator.gov.uk/trustees/signup/

If you have not yet done so, I urge you to spend a few hours on the Regulator's website. Go on, tell your boss it is essential trustee training!

If you wonder whether there is useful material you might be reading but are not aware of, ask your advisers – they should be plugged into professional networks that mean they know about the latest thinking and arguments. Don't let them keep it to themselves as specialist knowledge, learn too so that you can engage them in meaningful debate. This is particularly the case for LDI because it is arriving very quickly as a crucial part of trustee understanding.

Finally, if there is something you can't get hold of, try approaching the author directly. In my experience, most authors are extremely willing to share their published ideas and they will happily respond to an email request from a trustee. Rest assured, I wouldn't have been able to complete this book without great generosity from some of the people named above!

INDEX

LONGTAIL

**To order further copies call 020 7938 1975
or go to www.allyouneedtoknowguides.com**